SYMBOLS

PLANTS
CHARACTERS

Warmth-loving
plants

Spacing
in a row

Frost-resistant
plants

CULTIVATION
METHODS

Cold-loving
plants

Outside

In a
greenhouse

SOWING
METHODS

Under plastic
film

Planting tubers
and bulbs

In outdoor
beds

In seedbeds

CULTIVATION
METHODS

Outside

In a
greenhouse

Under plastic
film

VEGETABLES

Eva Pekárková

Illustrated by Petr Liška and Ester Polcarová

VEGETABLES
Original title Zelenina

Copyright © 1997 by Brio, spol. s r.o., Praha
© 1997 English edition Rebo Productions Ltd., London

Text by Eva Pekárková
Illustrated by Petr Liška and Ester Polcarová
Translated by Olga Kuthanová
Graphic layout and typesetting by Alfa
Colour separation by Repro plus, s.r.o.

ISBN 1 901094 57 x
Printed in Czech Republic.

CONTENTS

Why and how to grow vegetables   6
Brassicas   10
Leaf vegetables   28
Roots and tubers   58
Fruiting vegetables   84
Legumes   108
Onions and related vegetables   116
Index   126

Why and how to grow vegetables

During the course of evolution, man has become adapted to a mixed diet. Plant foods provide him with the basic nutrients (proteins, fats and sugars) as well as with important vitamins, minerals, enzymes, roughage, essential oils, and many protective and medicinal substances. The latter are found primarily in vegetables. They do not provide much energy, but are essential to health. They are found primarily in vegetables that are cooked briefly, so as to retain valuable substances that are often damaged by long cooking at high temperatures.

More and more people find satisfaction in growing their own vegetables, for a variety of reasons. For many amateur gardeners, it is the pleasure of having vegetables of a sweetness and freshness that cannot be had from shops. For others it is the knowledge that their home-grown vegetables do not contain harmful substances. Still others like the idea of growing unusual and exotic vegetables that are not commonly seen. There are also those who lay most value on a diversity of shapes and colours and the decorative appearance of certain species and varieties of vegetables. For some, the savings made on the family budget can be important too. Most often, however, it is the pleasure the gardener experiences when he can put on the table lovely vegetables from his own garden, vegetables he himself has sown, grown, and harvested.

How to grow vegetables

Vegetables require a sunny, sheltered position. They do best in non-compacting, moderately well-draining soil with a crumbly structure that contains sufficient humus, is easily worked, and at the same time best retains the nutrients and moisture required by the plants. The soil should be neutral to slightly acid (pH = 6-7). With some effort, such good-quality soil may be had within a few years. A decisive factor will be the use of organic manures. Using well-rotted compost is the most natural method.

Whereas some vegetables, such as brassicas, tomatoes, cucumbers, sweet peppers, and marrows, can be grown successfully after working farmyard manure into the soil in the autumn, in the case of others, mainly roots, legumes, onions and other allium species, applying fresh manure would result in a deterioration of the health and storage properties of the crops. Well-rotted compost as well as green manure (grass cuttings and the like worked into the soil before flowering) may be used for all vegetables.

Harvesting a wide variety of vegetables throughout the growing season may be achieved in a number of ways. First of all, new species are being introduced and varieties suitable for different environments are being developed by selective breeding. Some groups of vegetables include a wide range of varieties, with growing periods of different lengths. Brassicas and some leaf vegetables, for instance, include early varieties, i.e. quick-growing with a very short growing period, midseason varieties with a somewhat longer growing period, late varieties, and in some instances even hardy or winter varieties.

Vegetables are generally grown in outdoor beds. The best time for sowing or planting depends not just on the variety, but also on the conditions of the given location and given year. For this reason, in this book times are given as a 1- to 2-month range. Furthermore, to extend the growing season, some

Some vegetables are grown purely for ornamental reasons, e.g. ornamental gourd.

species (cress, small radish, bush beans, carrots) are sown at intervals, producing a number of successive crops. The sowing time also varies widely according to whether the seeds are sown outside, in a cold frame, in a plastic greenhouse, or in a heated or unheated glass greenhouse. The instructions on seed packets are the best guideline. Larger seeds (bean, pea, cucumber, melon, marrow) can be pregerminated so they will sprout more quickly. This is done at room temperature on a moist substrate in a flat dish covered with glass. Once they have grown a tiny root, the seeds are sown - always in moist soil.

An earlier harvest and more reliable yield may be attained by raising seedlings in pots and transplanting them to their final growing positions when they have reached the optimum stage of development. This is recommended for all vegetables that are to be grown in a greenhouse (lettuce, kohlrabi) and for those with a long growing period (Brussels sprouts, leek, cauliflower). Warmth-loving species (tomatoes, aubergines, sweet peppers, melons) are always raised in a protected environment. In this case seeds are sown thickly in a box, and the seedlings are pricked out into pots, plastic cups, or modules, which are plastic trays with numerous holes to hold soil and plants. Commercially grown plants are often blocked, i.e., grown in a compressed block of humus-rich soil. The simplest method of growing seedlings is to sow seeds thickly in a section of the bed

with fine, well-worked soil (seedbed). Of course this suits only those species that stand up well to being transplanted (brassicas, lettuce, leek). When the seedlings produce the first true leaves, they are carefully dug up and put out in their final growing positions at the required spacing.

For vegetables, an early harvest is always desirable. This may be speeded up even without permanent structures such as a cold frame or greenhouse. Vegetables may be harvested 1-2 weeks earlier by mulching in the case of

Mixed crop

Plants grown in a module

heat-loving plants (cucumbers, aubergines, sweet peppers, marrows, tomatoes) or by temporarily covering them with polytunnels or merely fencing them in with stakes and plastic film. In the case of low- growing vegetables (lettuce, small radish, radish, kohlrabi) covering them with perforated plastic film or fibrous film will serve this purpose very well.

Harvesting can be extended until winter by digging up grown plants before the winter and heeling them in, i.e., laying them close beside each other in a furrow in a sheltered bed or cold frame and covering their roots with soil.

When growing vegetables, it is important to use a system of crop rotation so that the same plant or a related species is not grown in the same place sooner than 3-4 years later. This will save the grower many problems with diseases and pests, it will eliminate the use of chemical controls, and it will benefit the plants, which will do better in soil that is not depleted of the nutrients that a particular crop most wants. The best method is to grow a preceding crop (a vegetable grown there before the present crop) and a following crop (a vegetable that is grown there in the autumn or the following year) belonging to different families (for that reason, the book lists the family along with the species or group of vegetable) or at least to different main groups of vegetables (leaf vegetables, legumes, etc.).

One of the new varieties developed by selective breeding is a cauliflower with purple florets.

Brassicas

The different kinds of brassicas are all varieties of a single species - *Brassica oleracea*, belonging to the cabbage family (Brassicaceae); only Chinese cabbage and pak choi belong to different species. Brassicas are typical crops of temperate regions, where they make up the largest part of vegetables consumed. They are one of the most important sources of vitamin C and are eaten raw, cooked, or made into sauerkraut, which increases their digestibility and vitamin content.

Cultivation

Brassicas do best in lowland areas with high atmospheric moisture. They are mostly large plants requiring large quantities of nutrients. Therefore they should be planted in good, well-fertilised soil, preferably dressed with compost. Their quality depends on a sufficient supply of moisture. They must be harvested in time so the heads do not split and florets and sprouts do not grow past their prime. Brassicas are cold-loving plants and do not tolerate high temperatures. Some are annuals (cauliflower, broccoli, Chinese cabbage and pak choi), others are biennial but are used the first year (cabbage, kale, kohlrabi). Frost-resistant varieties of cabbage, Savoy cabbage, Brussels sprouts, and kale can even overwinter outside. The parts that are eaten are the leaves, heads, fleshy inflorescences, and fleshy stems.

Most brassica species are highly variable in colour, shape, and size as well as in the time it takes them to mature. Vegetables can be harvested over a period of several months by choosing the right variety, location,

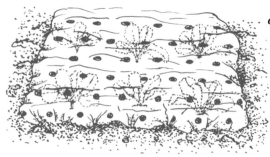

Early kohlrabi covered by perforated plastic film

Storing cabbage on a bed of straw

head is cut off and provide a new crop of young leaves. Storing suitable varieties of cabbage, Savoy cabbage, and kohlrabi makes it possible to have them throughout the year.

Diseases

All brassicas are affected by club root (*Plasmodiophora brassicae*), a serious disease that is best controlled by not growing them in the same place for several years. After being exposed to a cold spell in spring and during the long summer days some species, especially Chinese cabbage and pak choi, soon bolt without having formed the edible parts of the plant.

and sowing period. Kohlrabi, Savoy cabbage, Chinese cabbage and pak choi can also be forced in a greenhouse or under plastic film. Early varieties readily produce new growth after the

Ornamental kales form a ground rosette of leaves coloured green, shading off into purple or white

Cabbage

Brassica oleracea var. *capitata*

Cabbage is the commonest brassica in Europe, providing a year-round supply of fresh, stored, or pickled vegetables. It is easy to grow and the plants do well even in the harsher conditions of highland areas, where they are the principal vegetable crop (they even tolerate a light frost). There are two forms - green and red cabbage - developed in the past by selective breeding.

Cultivation and harvesting

The first to be harvested are the pointed varieties that have overwintered, only in maritime climates of course. Then early and midseason varieties of plants grown in modules or blocks. These varieties are used in the kitchen either raw or cooked. The latest to be harvested (before the first frost) are the varieties for making sauerkraut

and for winter storage. The seedlings of these varieties are grown in a seedbed (they should not be planted at higher temperatures), or else their seeds are sown directly in their final growing positions. Late varieties for winter storage of green and red cabbage will keep until late spring if stored just above freezing point.

Early varieties must be harvested in time so the heads do not split. In the

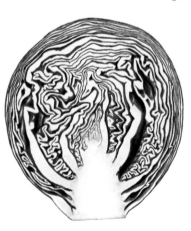

Section of a head of late red cabbage

Late cabbage can be sown directly in the outdoor bed - the seedlings are then thinned.

Overwintering pointed cabbage

case of storage varieties care must be taken that they are not bruised. Heads that are to be stored must be healthy and well cleaned. Modern F1 hybrids are noted for their highly uniform crops: all plants are the same size and mature at the same time. Like the leafy cabbages (see under Kale), early round types may be grown spaced closely together for harvesting of the young leaves.

There are also ornamental cabbages, which, like kale, form ground rosettes of leaves of a green colour, shading off into white or red.

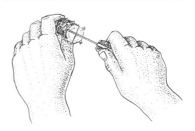

If after harvesting the heads of early varieties, a cross is cut on the remaining stump and it is given enough water, it will produce small heads that make fine salad greens.

Savoy cabbage

Brassica oleracea var. *sabauda*

Savoy cabbage differs from ordinary cabbage in being smaller (30-40 cm), having wrinkled and curly leaves, less compact heads, and greater resistance to frost. It tolerates temperatures as low as -10° C. It has a distinctive, very delicate flavour and freezes well.

Savoy cabbage is less widely grown than ordinary cabbage because its use in cookery is more limited. It is only eaten cooked. It has the advantage, however, that it can be grown throughout the year: there are varieties with small yellow heads that can be used for forcing and varieties that can be grown outside. The latter include varieties that are early, midseason, or late with strikingly dark-green leaves, as well as overwintering varieties planted in late summer and harvested as the first spring Savoy. Latest of all is the Langendijk type, which is not sown until April and can be stored until late spring. It differs from the other varieties, which are quite similar morphologically, in having much smoother leaves with a thick waxy coat and more compact heads so that it resembles a cross between Savoy and ordinary cabbage.

Savoy cabbage

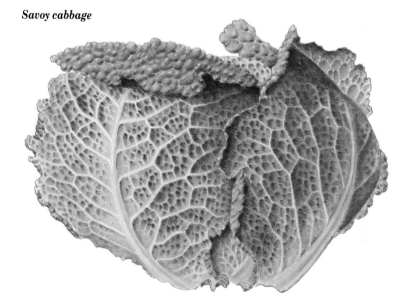

Plants in a block

Cultivation

Savoy cabbage has no special requirements and is easy to grow. In the case of early varieties, plants are grown in modules or blocks (the seeds are sown in the greenhouse as early as January or February). In the case of late varieties, seeds are sown in a bed (around April). The plants do not tolerate high temperatures. For overwintering and very early cultivation it is important to choose suitable varieties that do not have a tendency to bolt. In winter it is recommended to cover the plants with perforated plastic film or fibrous film.

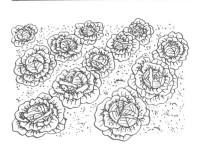

F1 hybrids make an attractive, uniform stand.

Cauliflower

Brassica oleracea var. botrytis

Of all brassicas, cauliflower is the most demanding crop. If you choose a suitable variety for the given environment, it may be harvested from spring till winter. Only certain southern European species, particularly Italian ones, tolerate higher temperatures. In hot climates, cauliflower is also grown in winter. It tolerates brief frosty spells of as low as -7° C, but the florets must be protected by tying the leaves together or by covering them with fibrous film. In the greenhouse, only early, smaller varieties are grown, that do not take up space for too long. The earliest varieties, so-called mini-cauliflowers, have heads smaller than the palm of the hand. Cauliflower plants grow to a height of 40 to 60 cm.

Cultivation

White-headed varieties are most popular. The snow-white colour of the head can be preserved by folding several leaves over it. In new varieties, the leaves tend to cover the head naturally. Recently, new varieties have been introduced with purple or vivid green heads (see picture on p. 9).

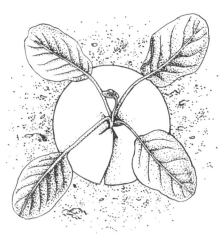

Collar of stiff paper placed around a young plant to prevent the Chlorophila brassicae fly from laying eggs at the base of the stem and its larvae from causing the gradual wilting and death of the plants.

Cauliflower is grown by sowing seeds in a box and pricking out the seedlings into modules or plastic cups. Alternatively, the seeds are sown in a seedbed. If the plants are dug up before winter together with the root and heeled in in a frame, the head may still grow to maturity. The heads consist of a very fleshy, highly branched inflorescence with undeveloped buds. A good-quality head is formed only if the plant has a permanent supply of sufficient nutrients and a regular supply of water. If the growth of the seedlings or young plants is checked by a shock of some sort, the plants' growth is halted as a result and only small, prematurely opening heads are formed.

Harvesting

Cauliflower is a very popular vegetable. It must be harvested while the heads are still firm and compact, otherwise they become tough and fibrous. They are eaten prepared in various ways, processed, and frozen.

Head of cauliflower

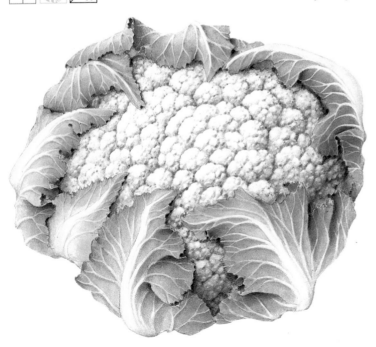

Broccoli

Brassica oleracea var. *cymosa*
and var. *asparagoides*

Two types of broccoli are grown: heading broccoli
and sprouting broccoli. The heading type (var. *cymosa*),
which resembles winter cauliflowers, is less widely
grown, and is restricted to maritime and southern
regions. It has a bigger head, takes longer to mature,
and is grown as an overwintering biennial, usually under
a protective covering, either fibrous film or a polytunnel.
More widely grown and more popular, however,
particularly in temperate regions, is sprouting broccoli
(var. *asparagoides*), which is an annual. It forms
a smaller, semi-compact head, usually green, although
there are also purple varieties that are even hardier.

*Main head of
sprouting broccoli*

Cultivation

Compared with cauliflower, broccoli is more tolerant of heat and moisture fluctuations and better withstands cold: it tolerates temperatures as low as -10° C. It also does well in less congenial climates, but it does not tolerate high temperatures. Its initial growth is relatively slow and it is therefore well-suited for intercropping, i.e. in alternating rows with other, faster-growing vegetables (kohlrabi, small radish, lettuce). The best distance between individual plants is 40 to 60 cm.

Harvesting

The heads of sprouting broccoli are harvested just before the buds open. The heads as well the fleshy stalks retain their quality and remain tender as long as they remain on the plant. Cutting off of the main head encourages the growth of smaller heads on the lateral shoots, thereby extending the harvesting period. These smaller heads are harvested with up to 10 cm of stalk and new ones continue to grow until winter. Once harvested, the small heads keep for a short while only. Broccoli is prepared by boiling shortly until the stalks are tender but still crisp. It also freezes well.

Small lateral head of broccoli

Seedlings do not stand up well to transplanting. They must be dug up from the seedbed with great care. Other good methods are growing them in modules or station sowing seeds and thinning the seedlings afterwards.

Kale

Brassica oleracea var. *acephala*
subvar. *laciniata*

Kale is one of the oldest brassicas and the most
frost-resistant. Shorter forms, up to 40 cm high, partly
covered by snow, overwinter best of all and survive
temperatures as low as -15° C. Kale is also resistant to
the most serious disease of the brassicas - club root
(*Plasmodiophora brassicae*).

Kale is undemanding and easy to
grow; in poorer soil and moisture
conditions, however, it does not grow
so well. The parts of the plant that are
eaten are the young leaves, which are
gathered on a cut-and-come-again
basis, beginning from the bottom of the
stem. The leaves of most varieties are
green, but some varieties have bluish-
red, reddish-brown, or variegated
leaves. Kale grows to a height of
30-120 cm, depending on the variety.

Kale's closest relative is leaf
cabbage (*Brassica oleracea* var.
acephala subvar. *plana*), which does
not form a head but grows only smooth
leaves on a tall, generally unbranched
stalk. The leaves are used as spinach.

*Leaf of a purple
variety*

40
70

Kale

Cultivation

Kale is sown directly outside (generally in April) in its final growing position and then thinned. Alternatively, the plants are grown in a bed or module. Young leaves are also obtained from thick sowings, from stalks that are cut back and then put out new leaves, or by growing under plastic film. Older leaves are tougher but become more delicate after exposure to frost. They are cooked as Savoy cabbage; young leaves are eaten raw. They freeze well. The leaves are also used to garnish foods.

Harvesting

To make harvesting easier in severe winters, the plants can be dug up in the autumn together with a rootball and heeled in a frame or in a cellar.

The plant does not form a head, but slightly or highly curled, very decorative leaves along the length of a non-branching or slightly branching stalk. Some forms resemble small palms.

Brussels sprouts

Brassica oleracea var. *gemmifera*

This is one of the youngest species of brassicas, created by intense selective breeding. Like kale, it is one of the most frost-resistant species. If the winter is not too severe or too dry and without snow, the plants tolerate temperatures even as low as -15° C. Earlier varieties do not overwinter as well as late varieties. A snow cover offers shorter varieties some protection against frost.

Cultivation

This vegetable needs a relatively long growing season and therefore it is advisable to raise the plants in a protected environment and then transplant them (seeds sown in April). For early autumn harvesting it is recommended to raise them in modules, for late harvesting they can be raised in a seedbed. The plants do not tolerate dry conditions and high temperatures. Brussels sprouts have high nutrient requirements, but if dressed with too much nitrogen fertiliser, the sprouts are not closed. Its

The F1 hybrid (left) produces firm sprouts of uniform size tightly together and regularly spaced along the entire length of the stalk. The non- hybrid plant (right) has irregular sprouts and because of its weaker root system it readily keels over.

*Top part
of Brussels
sprouts plant*

slow initial growth makes it highly suitable for intercropping with fast-growing vegetables (such as lettuce, kohlrabi, radish).

The sprouts develop in the axils of leaves that gradually turn yellow from the bottom upward. Yellow and diseased leaves should be removed during the growing season so they do not become the source of a fungal infection. This will also make for better air circulation. If plants are spaced farther apart, they produce large sprouts. Brussels sprouts reach a height of 40 to 100 cm, depending on the variety.

Harvesting

The best-quality sprouts measure 1.5 cm across, and are tightly closed and firm. They are gathered as they are ready, beginning from the bottom of the stalk so the upper sprouts can still mature. In addition to the green variety, there are also reddish-purple varieties that do not produce as many sprouts but are very tasty. All have a high nutritional value and have a better flavour after exposure to frost.

*To prevent toppling, soil is drawn up
round the roots up to the stem about
a month after planting.*

Kohlrabi

Brassica oleracea var. gongylodes

Kohlrabi is among the first spring vegetables. It is most widely grown in Central Europe. Highly prized is the fact that it can be forced in a greenhouse, covered by plastic film, grown outside for early, summer, as well autumn harvesting, and also stored for a lengthy period.

The edible portion of kohlrabi is the round, fleshy, swollen stem topped by long-stalked leaves. Cultivated varieties are whitish-green or purple and differ in the length of the growing season. The fleshy stems are eaten raw or cooked.

Cultivation

It is necessary to choose suitable varieties for the given environment and the length of the growing period. Harvesting of early varieties may be speeded up by raising plants in blocks or modules (in March); autumn varieties may be sown directly in the outdoor bed and then thinned. The plants must be fed and watered regularly. If planted very close together, kohlrabi does not form properly developed stems. Stress caused by dry conditions and insufficient nutrients as well as belated harvesting causes the fleshy stems to become woody.

Kohlrabi does not tolerate high temperatures but it does not mind a brief frosty spell. Early varieties have a smaller, flattened fleshy stem, less than 10 cm wide, with very delicate

Outdoors, early varieties respond very well to floating mulches of perforated plastic film or fibrous film (detail to the right).

Early purple kohlrabi

The late variety 'Gigant'

leaves. Seedlings must not be exposed to temperatures just above freezing point as this would cause lengthening of the stems and they would soon bolt.

Kohlrabi reach a height of 30 to 40 cm, depending on the variety.

Early kohlrabies grow quickly and have fewer and smaller leaves and are therefore suitable for intercroppping with other vegetables.

Chinese cabbage and pak choi

Brassica pekinensis and *Brassica chinensis*

Chinese cabbage and pak choi are excellent East Asian vegetables adapted to the monsoon climate of their native habitat with balanced moisture and heat conditions. The site and cultivation requirements of the two species are the same. The pale green heads of Chinese cabbage, composed of non-pruinose, faintly curly leaves, are cigar-shaped or with a rounded tip. Pak choi differs from Chinese cabbage primarily in that it does not form a firm head but a semi-erect rosette of smooth, glossy leaves. Both species are 30 to 50 cm high.

Chinese cabbage

This cabbage grows very fast. It is sensitive to temperatures just above freezing point, dry weather, insufficient nutrients, and long daylight, which soon cause it to bolt without forming a head.

In temperate climates with long summer days it must therefore be sown very early (in February) in a greenhouse or, alternatively, in an outdoor bed as a follow-on crop, from the second half of July. It tolerates a mild frost when fully mature. The seeds are either

After the mature head is cut off about 2.5 cm above the soil, the remaining portion will produce several smaller leaf rosettes.

Young leaves of pak choi are also obtained by growing the plants close together; they will sprout after the plants are cut off close to the ground.

Chinese cabbage

Pak choi

station sown and the plants then thinned to a spacing of 25 to 30 cm, or the plants are raised in a module.

This cabbage is generally eaten raw in salads, mainly in winter.

Pak choi

This cabbage was introduced into Europe only in recent decades and is less common than Chinese cabbage. The parts used are primarily its wide, fleshy leaf stalks and midribs. They are used in the same way as Chinese cabbage.

Leaf vegetables

The successful growth of the leaves, in this group the part that is eaten, depends on a good supply of nutrients and regular watering. Also important is sufficient light, influenced not only by the time of cultivation and the site but also by the distance between the cultivated plants. Leaf vegetables provide the earliest and latest harvest of the year - periods when fresh vegetables are in shortest supply - as well as the largest amount of vitamin C and provitamin A.

Classification

According to their use, leaf vegetables are classified into: the lettuce group (lettuce, endive, chicory, garden cress, watercress, lamb's lettuce), the spinach group (spinach, orache, Swiss chard leaves, New Zealand spinach), and the stem group (Swiss chard stems, celery). Set somewhat apart by the fact that they are perennials are rhubarb, cardoon, and asparagus. Typical leaf vegetables are in the main cold-loving annuals and are therefore grown primarily in spring and autumn. Some species (lamb's lettuce) and varieties (some lettuces, spinach) are frost-resistant and grown as overwintering plants. In summer, high temperatures do not

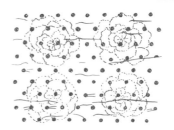

Lettuce beneath perforated plastic film

agree with them, nor do the long hours of daylight, which cause them to bolt. As they are content with low temperatures, they are ideal for very early forcing in a greenhouse, polytunnel or frame. Furthermore, their low height makes it possible

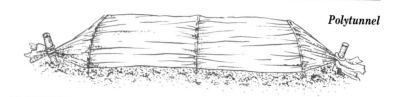

Polytunnel

to have an earlier crop by covering them with polytunnels or floating mulches of perforated plastic film or fibrous film.

Cultivation

Their rapid growth and short growing period make it possible to grow them before the main crop (e.g. tomatoes, vegetable marrows), after the main crop (early potatoes, peas), or also in mixed crops (in alternating rows, e.g. with celery, celeriac, or leek).

Lettuces spoil readily and cannot be stored. During transport and brief storage they require cool conditions and protection against evaporation. In the case of plants that make heads, it is also possible to consume the individual leaves from thick sowings or resprouting from stumps.

New Zealand spinach

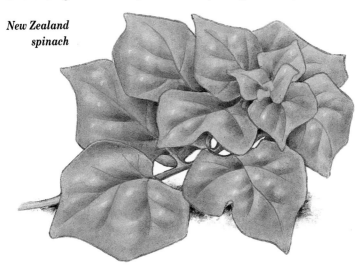

Trimming the root of chicory for forcing

Lettuce seed - longitudinally ribbed and pointed at both ends - differs markedly from the seed of the similar endive and chicory which is topped by a crown at one end (see endive).

Lettuce

Lactuca sativa

Lettuce is extraordinarily variable morphologically as well as in the character of its development. Its outstanding characteristic is that it is eaten raw. It is hardy, cold-loving and even frost-resistant; in summer it bolts. It belongs to the composite family (Asteraceae).

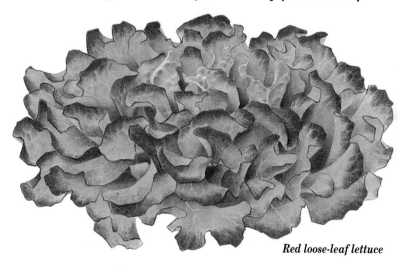

Red loose-leaf lettuce

Most popular is cabbage lettuce (var. *capitata*), widely grown for spring and winter-forcing as well as for planting outside for early, late, autumn, or spring (after overwintering) harvesting. It responds very well to being grown under floating mulches of perforated plastic film or fibrous film as well as under polytunnels. Least likely to bolt are summer crisphead (iceberg) lettuces with prominent ribs and crinkly-edged glossy leaves (*jaggeri* type) and loose leaf lettuces (var. *secalina*) that do not form a head and have silky-fine,

often curly leaves harvested either by cutting off the whole plants or by picking the leaves on a cut-and-come-again basis as required. Of all the lettuces, crisphead (iceberg) lettuces are the least prone to wilting.

Cultivation

Early lettuces are always raised in a protected environment; summer, autumn, and overwintering lettuces are grown from plants raised in a seedbed or else from seeds sown

Long heads of cos lettuce - romaine (var. romana) have a mildly bitter flavour and are therefore blanched by tying them in order to eliminate the bitterness. They are grown mainly in Southern Europe.

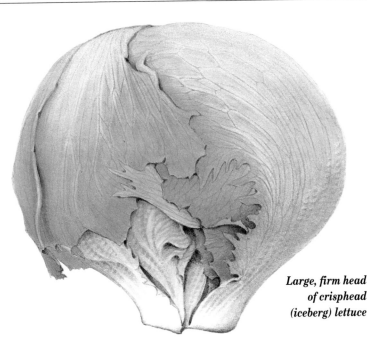

Large, firm head of crisphead (iceberg) lettuce

directly in the outdoor bed, the plants later being thinned to 20 to 30 cm apart. The earliest harvest of leaves is obtained from thickly sown, curly, loose leaf lettuces. Cabbage lettuces become bitter in dry weather and when they bolt, and fully grown crisphead (iceberg) lettuces rot inside in hot weather.

Loose-leaf as well as cabbage lettuces can be grown successfully in containers. Lettuces reach a height of 10 to 20 cm.

Chicory

Cichorium intybus var. *foliosum*

The heads and shoots of chicory differ from lettuces in having a mildly bitter flavour. Chicory's most prized characteristic is that it grows to maturity and is harvested in winter, when fresh lettuce is in short supply. It is highly resistant to diseases, pests, as well as light frosts. It reaches a height of 30 to 40 cm.

Cultivation

Chicory is primarily used for forcing, producing so-called witloof chicory. This is grown in a bed from seeds sown in late spring, with subsequent thinning of the plants. The roots are lifted in late autumn and stored in a cellar after the tops have been cut off 2-3 cm from the crown. Other chicories are grown from seeds sown directly outside in July so they do not bolt. There are two kinds: green- leafed and red-leafed.

Forced witloof chicory chicon

Bucket with forced blanched chicons

Forcing

The chicory roots are forced gradually from December till March. They should be at least 3 cm thick. Trim, put into a bucket, and cover with water to two thirds of their height. Cover the bucket with black plastic film, and tie it firmly around the bucket to exclude all light. Keep the bucket at a temperature of 14-20° C. Firm blanched chicons will appear 2-3 weeks later. Cut them off with a piece of the neck, so they do not fall apart. Store in a dark place or dark wrapping so they do not become green and bitter.

The seeds of sweet green-leafed Zuckerhut are sown directly outside and the plants are thinned to a spacing of 30 x 30 cm. The heads tolerate temperatures as low as -8˚C. When the head is cut off in time, the stem will produce new leaves that can be used as a salad green.

Radicchio forms round heads of red and white leaves. It is grown the same way as Zuckerhut.

Endive

Cichorium endivia

Endive forms ground rosettes of leaves about 10-15 cm high. The leaves are tougher than those of lettuces but mildly bitter like those of its close relative, chicory. The bitter substances are good for your health. Endive acquires a delicate flavour by blanching in the absence of light. Endives are less widely grown than lettuces.

Summer curly endive

Cultivation

Endive is either sown directly in an outdoor bed, with subsequent thinning of the plants, or it is raised in a seedbed or in modules. It is generally grown in open ground with a distance of 30 to 40 cm between the individual plants. A notable characteristic of endive is that it is more rot-resistant than lettuce. This

The seeds of endive and chicory are distinguished from those of lettuces by the crown at one end of the elongated seed.

Winter endive (escarole)

is particularly prized in the broad-leaved winter endive called escarole (var. *latifolia*) when growing endive in late autumn and overwintering it in a greenhouse. The plants tolerate temperatures as low as -9° C. Escarole for late harvesting is sown from July onwards, not before. Lifted plants can be matured and blanched within 2-3 weeks, with leaves tied and turned upside down, in a cellar or frame. Summer, curly endives (var. *crispum*) with finely jagged leaves have a shorter growing period; they must be harvested in time so they do not bolt. They can be partly blanched by covering the centre of the rosette with a plate or piece of cardboard or by covering the whole plant with black plastic film. In 10 days, the covered leaves will become pale, more delicate and will lose their bitter flavour. Blanched plants will not keep long, however.

Young endive plants, like young lettuce, are put out so the heart of the leaf rosette is at the level of the soil surface and is not covered by earth.

Lamb's lettuce and Dandelion

Valerianella olitoria and *Taraxacum officinale*

Lamb's lettuce and dandelion were originally weeds; therefore they have no demanding requirements and are easy to grow. They make excellent, nutritious and tasty raw out-of-season salads.

Lamb's lettuce

Lamb's lettuce is a cold-loving, frost-resistant plant, 5 to 10 cm high, that bolts in summer. These characteristics have made it a salad green of the autumn and above all the winter season. Lamb's lettuce is sown either as early as possible in spring or in July for autumn harvesting and in the autumn for overwintering. The plants tolerate frost and therefore usually overwinter outside, which is their most prized characteristic. To enable easy harvesting throughout the winter, they are covered by, for instance, polytunnels or glass. The plants are small, and therefore the crop must be kept free from weeds.

Lamb's lettuce

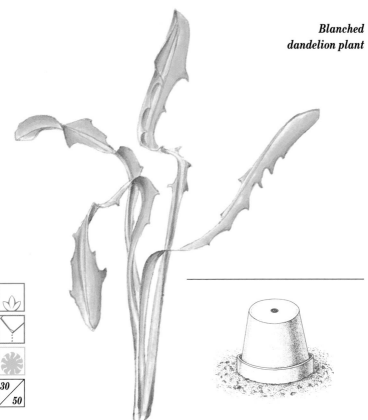

*Blanched
dandelion plant*

Dandelion

The leaves of dandelion are used as a very early raw spring salad of slightly bitter flavour. The developing leaves should be blanched by excluding light, as otherwise they would be tough and too bitter. Cultivated forms have large 20 to 40 cm long leaves that show some signs of heading and are less bitter. Even weedy plants, however, can be blanched. The leaves are picked as required. Dandelion is sown either early in spring or in the autumn for spring blanching.

*Dandelion leaves are blanched by
covering the seedlings in spring
with a bell jar or flower pot or by
tying the leaves and covering them
to exclude light.*

Plastic shelter

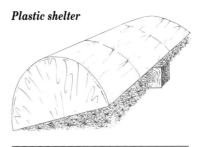

Garden cress and Watercress

Lepidium sativum and *Nasturtium officinale*

Garden cress and watercress (cabbage family - Brassicaceae) are delicate herbs with a pleasant peppery flavour. The young plants and shoots are used raw - by themselves or combined with other greens.

Garden cress

Garden cress starts growing at temperatures as low as 5° C and does so at a rapid pace. It can be grown not only in a bed but above all in a flowerpot and even without soil, indoors in a dish on a piece of damp cloth, and even in the middle of winter. The newly formed young plants can be cut for use with scissors as soon as 10-14 days after sowing. The delicate incised leaves contain vitamin C. Chopped raw garden cress enhances the taste of salads, sandwich spreads, meats, as well as cheeses. The plants quickly bolt as the days lengthen, which is why they are grown only from seed sown very early in spring or late in summer for autumn harvesting. Cress requires moist conditions. It reaches a height of 20 to 30 cm.

Watercress

Watercress grows in clear streams from lowland areas to high altitudes. The prostrate shoots, 60 to 80 cm long, are submerged in water and only the growing points protrude

Clump of garden cress grown on damp cloth in a dish

8 / 10

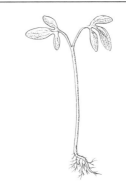

Young garden cress plant of harvesting size grown in a dish

Watercress

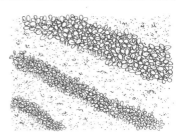

Young foliage of garden cress is obtained by sowing into open ground at intervals of about 10 days. Plants are harvested when 5-15 cm high.

above the surface. It grows wild or is cultivated for its sprigs used fresh to flavour soups and many other dishes.

A clump of watercress is established in August by planting rooted sideshoots and gradually covering them with water after they have taken hold, to a depth of 2-40 cm.

Watercress is harvested mainly in winter, from October till May. It can also be grown in a dish placed in a bowl of water. The sprigs keep well in cold water or sprinkled with crushed ice.

Sprigs of watercress, harvested when 6-8 cm long, will be more delicate if pushed underwater.

Chinese mustard and Purslane

Brassica juncea and *Portulaca oleracea*

Chinese mustard (cabbage family - Brassicaceae) and purslane (purslane family - Portulacaceae) are less common, but are a pleasant addition to the assortment of salad greens.

Chinese mustard

Chinese mustard forms ground rosettes 20 to 30 cm high, of pale green, dark green, or purple-tinged, smooth or slightly curly leaves with fleshy leaf stalks - it is grown mainly for the latter. For harvesting the leaves the seeds must be sown either very early in spring or not before July, as in summer it bolts before forming a proper leaf rosette. In warmer areas it overwinters; purple-leafed varieties tolerate temperatures as low as -10° C. The leaves are used raw in salads but are also pickled or canned. The flower stems are also used in salads, as are the fleshy roots of certain varieties.

Chinese mustard

Green purslane

Purslane

There are two sorts: green purslane and golden purslane. Golden purslane is more attractive and is used in salads, green purslane has thinner leaves but the plants are more robust. Purslane is a prostrate plant, 20 to 30 cm high, with fleshy leaves. The whole plants are harvested, or, alternatively, the stems are clipped for use as required.

Purslane requires sun and a sheltered situation. Frost destroys the foliage. In cold climates it is raised in a protected environment in spring; in summer the seeds are sown at intervals directly in their final growing positions. When harvesting, leave the basal parts of the stems, so they can put out new growth, and remove flowers. The development of the plants can be speeded up by covering them with plastic film or glass but it is necessary to provide sufficient air circulation.

Mustard is one of the vegetables that can be successfully grown in a container, by itself or together with other species. It is harvested on a cut-and-come-again basis by pulling off the leaves.

Swiss chard

Beta vulgaris var. cicla

Unlike sugar beet (var. *altissima*), turnip (var. *vulgaris*) and beetroot (var. *crassa*), all of which belong to the same family and the same genus (goosefoot family or Chenopodiaceae), the edible part of Swiss chard is the leaves; the root is not used because it remains small and non-fleshy. The leaves are upright, the leaf blades glossy, slightly fleshy, and highly wrinkled. All parts of the plant have a typical beet flavour due to the presence of betaine.

Varieties

One group comprises leaf forms with relatively thin leaf stalks; the leaf blades, coloured pale green, dark green, and red, are used as delicate 'perennial spinach'. The other group comprises forms with fleshy leaf stalks and leaf ribs that are used for cooking. There are also transitional forms between the two groups.

Cultivation and harvesting

The plants are robust (they grow to a height of 50 to 70 cm) and therefore require good soil and sufficient moisture. They are grown from seed. Swiss chard is harvested by breaking off the individual leaves throughout the growing season. In the case of leafy forms the young plants may likewise be clipped repeatedly. In autumn the plants

Leaf of white-stalked Swiss chard

Like all other beets, Swiss chard forms irregular glomerules with several cavities, a single seed in each of them.

When sown, the glomerule will produce a clump of 3-4 seedlings that must be thinned. Swiss chard is very susceptible to damage by frost as well as by caked soil when sprouting.

endure freezing temperatures as low as -12° C. Once dug up, the plants can be stored in a cellar or greenhouse and in spring they will yield a very early crop of leaves. In warmer areas, Swiss chard can be sown in summer and then overwintered after earthing up.

Stalk chard is self-blanching and forms fleshy snow-white leaf stalks; a highly decorative red form is also grown. The leaf stalks and leaf blades are used separately - the former cooked like asparagus, sautéed, or baked; the latter prepared like spinach.

Red-stalked Swiss chard

Celery

Apium graveolens var. dulce

In areas with uniform moisture and heat conditions, preference is given to growing celery, whereas in continental climates the preferred type is celeriac. Compared with celeriac, celery has only a small root, which is not eaten. The leafy tops, on the other hand, are highly developed, 40-60 cm tall. The broad fleshy leaf stalks are eaten raw or cooked; the sap from the stalks is also used. The plants do not form seeds until the second year of growth; the seed is ground for use as seasoning. Celery belongs to the carrot family (Daucaceae).

Cultivation and harvesting

The plants require a good, balanced supply of nutrients and moisture. They grow slowly at first and do not tolerate severe frost; low temperatures above freezing point cause them to bolt. They are grown from seeds sown early (in February) in a greenhouse. The seedlings are tiny and need to be pricked out into a module or blocks. Later they are planted 30 to 40 cm apart. Celery is harvested in late summer and autumn. Plants that are not harvested may be lifted before the first frost and stored in a frame or cellar.

Stalks can be eaten only if they are blanched. Some types are self-blanching, in other words they do not have to be kept in the dark, and their leaf blades, stalks, and leaf ribs are

Prepared stalks with leaves removed

Gradual wrapping of green celery in paper to exclude light

Self-blanching celery

crisp, juicy and sweet. When planted closer together, the mutual shading of the leaves improves the quality of the stalks. Green varieties must be blanched to be edible. They are planted in trenches and light is gradually excluded by wrapping them in paper, followed by earthing them up but never higher than the leaf base - the leaf tops must remain exposed to allow the access of light and continuing growth of the plants. The stalks have a delicate, pungent flavour and pronounced aroma.

Sweet fennel

Foeniculum vulgare var. dulce

This type of fennel is most closely related to the fennel used as flavouring. It forms swollen stem bases above ground. These have a strong aniseed aroma and are used raw or cooked. It requires a sheltered site but otherwise does well in climates ranging from temperate to subtropical. One thing it does not tolerate is the soil drying out.

Cultivation

Sweet fennel, belonging to the carrot family (Daucaceae), is a vegetable that can be grown as a second crop (after lettuce, small radishes, early potatoes) because the seeds must not be sown until June or July, to prevent bolting. It also bolts readily after the shock of transplanting. It is difficult to transplant and is therefore grown from station-sown seeds, the plants being thinned to 20 to 25 cm apart, or, alternatively, by raising them in a module; the plants should have four leaves at the most when set into the soil.

The laterally compressed swollen stem bases are formed by the fleshy, longitudinally ridged leaf bases clasping the stem. No other vegetable has anything like this. As they mature, the swollen stem bases become round instead of elongated. The Bologna, Sicilian, and Palermo varieties with shorter stem and wide leaf bases are eaten raw, whereas the Florence varieties with longer stalks are cooked.

The swollen stem bases become more delicate and sweet if they are partly blanched by earthing up the plants. The best time for this is when the stem bases measure about 5 cm across. Mulching with moisture-retentive organic matter is also recommended. Fennel is practically disease- and pest-free. The plants reach a height of 40 to 50 cm.

If the mature plant is cut off 2.5 cm above the ground, young thread-like leaves will grow around the edges, making a good green kitchen herb.

Young plant with swollen stem bases, which are still elongated

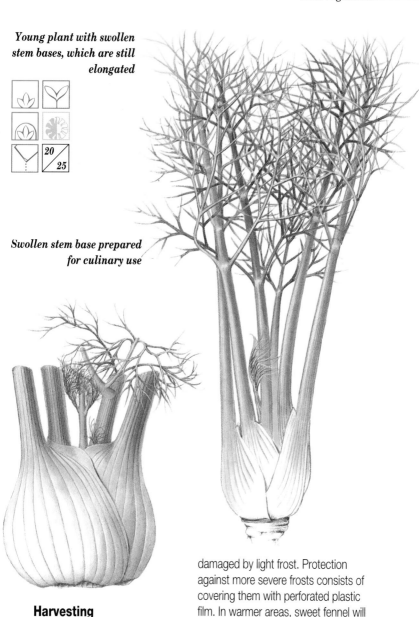

Swollen stem base prepared for culinary use

Harvesting

The swollen stem bases are harvested in autumn before the first frost. Adult plants, however, are not damaged by light frost. Protection against more severe frosts consists of covering them with perforated plastic film. In warmer areas, sweet fennel will overwinter if it is well covered with straw or leaves. It can be stored only by heeling in in a frame or cellar. Plants are usually harvested by pulling them up.

Cardoon

Cynara cardunculus

Botanically, cardoons are closely related to the similar artichokes; both belong to the composite family (Asteraceae). They have the same requirements but are more robust. They are grown for the fleshy leaf stalks and leaf ribs. During the growing season the plants require warmth, sufficient nutrients, and moisture.

Cultivation

Though cardoons are perennials, they are generally grown as annuals raised from seed. They require plenty of space, which is why seedlings are put out about one metre apart. They overwinter outside but because they are susceptible to damage by frost they must be provided with a good protective covering.

Cardoons are vigorous plants reaching a height of 100 to 120 cm with attractive leaves as well as flowers. The leaves are highly divided, up to 1 m long, felted on the underside, with broad fleshy stalks and ribs. Older species have short hard thorns on the leaves, more recent varieties, currently popular, however, are thornless.

Blanching

The leaf stalks and ribs need to be blanched in order to soften, become more delicate, and lose their bitter flavour. Blanching usually starts in August or September and ends before

If cardoons are not grown in soil that is too poor or too dry, the blanched leaf stalks are extraordinarily delicate and tasty. They are harvested by cutting off individual blanched leaves just above the ground. Only the stalks are used (cooked like asparagus); the leaf blades are removed.

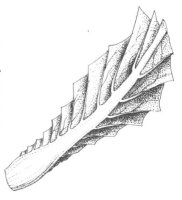

*The inflorescence is a head of
purple flowers resembling
those of artichokes but
smaller. It is not eaten.*

the first frost. For blanching, adult plants
are tied loosely together at the top,
wrapped in straw or black plastic film,
and earth is hilled up around the base
of the plants, leaving the leaf tops
exposed to enable the plants to
continue to grow. The wrapping should
not be too thick so the plants do not
rot. Another possibility is to dig up the
plants in autumn, tie the leaves at the
top and store them in the cellar. They
are then harvested during the winter.

Rhubarb

Rheum x *cultorum*

Rhubarb is one of the earliest vegetables. It is grown for its large stalks, which are used as cooked fruit. Some species are important medicinal plants. It belongs to the buckwheat family (Polygonaceae).

Rhubarb is a robust, perennial plant, up to 60 cm high, that spreads out over the years. It produces large pink buds very early in spring, one of the first plants to do so. The leaves have large, slightly curly blades, and long, fleshy stalks coloured green, reddish or red. In spring, the leaf stalks, or 'sticks', provide the first material for making compotes, jam and pie fillings. In addition to vitamins, they contain oxalic acid, which is why rhubarb dishes are advised against in the case of some diseases. The leaves contain so much oxalic acid that they are not used for culinary purposes or even for feed.

Cultivation and harvesting

Rhubarb will grow even in a shaded position, but requires sufficient moisture and nutrients in the soil. It is generally propagated by the division of clumps in the autumn, for varieties do not breed fully true when propagated from seed.

Stalks are not pulled the first year after planting, so the plants will become stronger. The flowers are removed repeatedly as they appear, so their growth does not weaken the plants.

More delicate and earlier stalks may be obtained by forcing in the absence of light. Fully grown stalks are harvested, beginning with the oldest, by pulling - catching hold of the base of the stalk, twisting it and simultaneously pulling it up and out. Harvesting ends in April. Enough leaves should be left on the plant to enable photosynthesis, so the plant can continue to grow. Plants may be left in place for 10 years or even longer.

Forcing

The plant is dug up in autumn and moved to a greenhouse; alternatively, it is left outside with the bed covered to exclude light. Plants may also be covered with barrels surrounded by strawy manure that heats the inside. They are harvested after about four weeks.

Forcing rhubarb outside in the bed

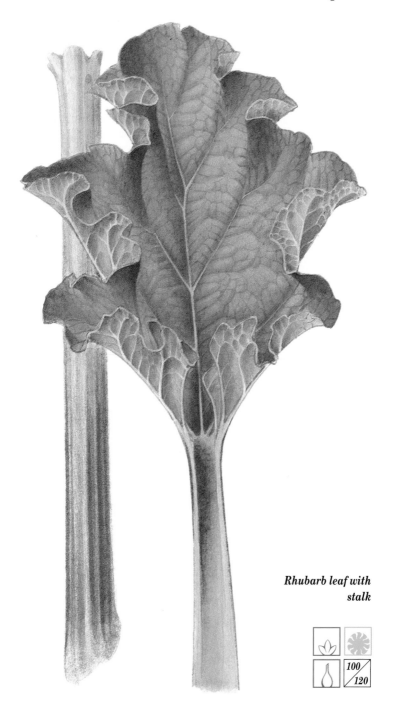

*Rhubarb leaf with
stalk*

Asparagus

Asparagus officinalis

Asparagus (lily family - Liliaceae) is called a royal vegetable because it used to be considered a special delicacy available only to the wealthy. Though it grows wild in Europe, growing cultivated varieties is not at all easy. The part that is eaten is the young fleshy shoots that are harvested in spring when they appear above the surface of the soil. They are used in salads, as a starter, in soups, as well as as a side dish, and are often canned.

Asparagus is a dioecious plant, 100 to 150 cm tall. When ripe, female plants may be identified by the red berries. Male plants usually make fewer young shoots but these are much thicker and therefore more highly prized. This characteristic has been selectively bred into the F1 hybrids, which have thick shoots of equal size.

In addition to the traditional varieties whose young shoots are blanched by earthing up, varieties with green shoots are becoming increasingly popular. These have a much greater vitamin content. Their fine, delicate, fibreless structure, obtained without blanching, is the result of selective breeding.

Male and female plants

60 / 120

Cultivation

First to grow from the large clump of roots are fleshy shoots which later develop into tall, slender stems with needle-like leaves. Asparagus is grown from seed sown in spring, usually into modules, and raised for 1-2 years before being put in a trench 60-120 cm apart and earthed up. Dry shoots are cut off and removed in autumn.

Planting young asparagus plants. The roots are spread out and gradually covered with soil, leaving only a small part of the shoot exposed.

Bunch of green shoots

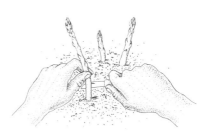

Harvesting asparagus shoots

Harvesting

Asparagus is not harvested until the second or third season. Shoots are cut with a knife about 15 cm below the tip after pulling away the soil. When doing this, care must be taken not to damage neighbouring shoots that are growing below the surface. If they are well fertilised, the plants can remain in the same spot for 15 to 20 years.

Spinach

Spinacia oleracea

Spinach is the most typical vegetable of the spinach group. Its leaves are used cooked in various ways as a side dish and may also be eaten raw as a salad green. They contain vitamins, proteins, and minerals, as well as oxalic acid, which is detrimental in some diets. Spinach belongs to the goosefoot family (Chenopodiaceae).

Most common nowadays are varieties with slightly wavy, upright leaves. There are also varieties with leaves that are practically smooth, however, and ones with highly wrinkled, fleshy leaves. Older varieties of spinach were dioecious, i.e. bearing male and female flowers on different plants. More recent varieties and F1 hybrids are mostly monoecious, so that the plants

In summer, if water and nutrients are in short supply and plants are set too close together, spinach soon bolts without forming the typical leaf rosette. Bolting plants are slightly bitter and cannot be used.

Young leaf

Spinach plant

have the desired uniform development. They grow 10 to 20 cm high.

Cultivation

The growth of the plants is rapid and they require sufficient moisture and nutrients. They are grown in cool weather at three different times: seeds may be sown in early spring for harvesting in May, in August for harvesting in autumn, and in September for overwintering and harvesting in April. Seedlings must be thinned to 20-30 cm. Spinach is not sown from April till July because it would bolt. It is important to choose suitable varieties for sowing at different times.

The hardiest varieties are those with toothed leaves resembling those of dandelion. Their drawback is a lower yield and prickly seeds that make sowing more difficult; the seeds of round-seeded varieties are not prickly.

Harvesting and use

Spinach freezes very well; frozen, finely chopped spinach is available throughout the winter and to a great extent is taking the place of spring forcing and winter cultivation under cover for the harvesting of fresh leaves. Spinach is frost-resistant, making it possible to harvest young fresh leaves, mainly for use as a salad green, by repeated cutting as required even in a mild winter as long as access to the leaves is made possible with plastic cloches or plastic film.

Orache and New Zealand spinach

Atriplex hortensis and *Tetragonia tetragoniodes*

Orache and New Zealand spinach produce leaves that are excellent cooked and prepared like spinach.

Orache

This is an annual plant of the goosefoot family, with normal to little branching, reaching a height of up to 150 cm. There are two forms - pale green and reddish purple; the latter is unusually attractive throughout the entire growing season.

Orache is an undemanding plant that is easy to grow and its growth is rapid. In dry, poor soil and if set close together, however, the plants do not grow as tall. In the garden it readily seeds and becomes naturalised. The seeds are sown early in spring because plants from later sowings bolt. Seeds may also be sown for autumn harvesting. The tastiest leaves for cooking as spinach are ones from young plants. Leaves can also be harvested from older plants, however.

New Zealand spinach

This is a prostrate, spreading plant, no more than 10-15 cm high, belonging to the Aizoaceae family. Grown for its fleshy leaves and shoots, it is one of the few vegetables native to the southern hemisphere. It does best at high summer temperatures and can be harvested practically all through the summer. It is an excellent substitute for spinach at a time when true spinach bolts. Growth is slow at first and therefore it can be intercropped with fast- growing vegetables (e.g. small radishes, kohlrabi). The large-leafed and highly branched plants take up a lot of space (plants should be planted 40 to 60 cm apart) and form a continuous stand. They are destroyed by frost.

The hard pericarp of the tetrahedral fruit absorbs water only very slowly and for that reason must be soaked so it swells before sowing.

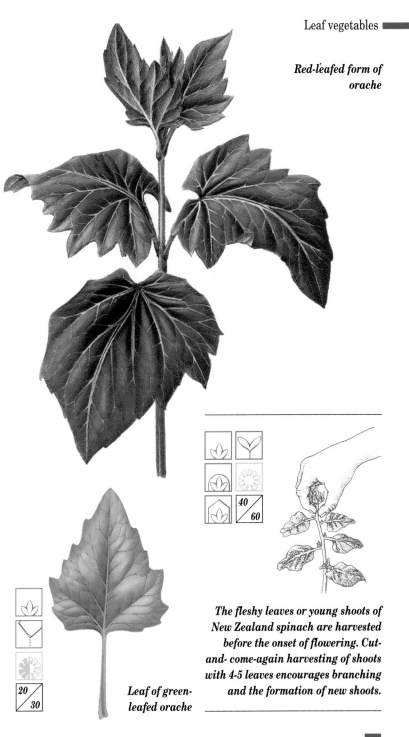

Red-leafed form of orache

Leaf of green-leafed orache

The fleshy leaves or young shoots of New Zealand spinach are harvested before the onset of flowering. Cut-and-come-again harvesting of shoots with 4-5 leaves encourages branching and the formation of new shoots.

57

Roots and tubers

This group of vegetables used for culinary and medicinal purposes comprises the underground fleshy and enlarged roots or tubers. In the main, they belong to three botanical families: the carrot family (Daucaceae) - carrot, parsley, celeriac, and parsnip; the cabbage family (Brassicaceae) - radish, small radish, turnip, swede; and the composite family (Asteraceae) - scorzonera, salsify and Jerusalem artichoke.

Cultivation

For the proper development of the underground parts, the plants need nourishing soil that is loose, non-compacting, without stones, and uniformly moist. Deep soil is important mainly for species with long roots - scorzonera, parsley, carrot, radish. They do not tolerate fresh organic manure because it increases their susceptibility to diseases and reduces their keeping quality. They are cold-loving plants and the seeds are therefore sown very early in spring (especially plants of the carrot family). Only the sprouting seedlings of beetroot and celeriac are susceptible to damage by frost. Parsnip, parsley, scorzonera, horseradish, and Jerusalem artichoke overwinter in the open.

The seeds of some species (carrot, celeriac, parsley) are so small that they are generally sold as pellets to facilitate sowing. Most species are biennials that may bolt already in the first year as a result of cold conditions at the initial stage of their development. Most susceptible are celeriac and beetroot. Early varieties, such as carrot,

Digging up mulched celeriac

Harvesting young carrots

Horseradish is a very pungent which is why it used as a condiment

Beetroot is a popular and attractive root vegetable

small radish, summer radish and turnip, must be harvested in time so the roots do not split and the edible parts do not lose their fine structure. A tried and tested method is forcing in a frame or polytunnel, or under a floating mulch of perforated plastic film.

Storing

All species of root and tuberous vegetables can be stored and keep very well, thus making an important contribution to the winter diet.

For storing it is of course necessary to select suitable varieties that have been fertilised with care. Roots and tubers are highly nourishing mainly because of their starch and protein content. Some also contain significant amounts of substances important to health such as vitamins, inulin for diabetics, essential oils that are important for digestion, as well as diuretic substances.

Carrot

Daucus carota

This is the most important root vegetable. It is native to Europe, which is why it does well there. It has many culinary uses, raw as well as cooked. It is available practically throughout the year, as it can be forced, grown in open ground throughout the entire growing season, stored (it keeps well), frozen, and canned. Moreover it is the main source of carotene (provitamin A) and other vitamins.

Early varieties as well as varieties for forcing have smaller, blunt-tipped, round or cylindrical roots. Later varieties, grown for storing, are larger and taper to a point. They are best stored in boxes sandwich-fashion in damp sand. They can also be stored in plastic bags.

Cultivation

Carrots are easily grown in well-worked nourishing soil; on shallow or stony soils, the roots fork and become deformed. Carrot seeds are small and rough. The first sowing starts early in spring (even in February) because the seeds germinate very slowly and need to take advantage of the winter moisture. Carrots tolerate light frost. Their development may also be speeded up by temporarily covering them with perforated plastic film. Seedlings must be thinned to 7-20 cm apart. The uprooted seedlings should be removed so they do not attract carrot fly (*Psila rosa*), the most serious

Late carrot for storing

carrot pest. The female flies lay eggs on young plants, these develop into larvae that tunnel into the roots, causing them to become unpleasantly wormy. The carrot crop can be protected by covering it with a special fine netting.

The early varieties that are eaten when they are young and tender are sown in spring and late summer. They should be harvested in time, so the roots do not split. The late varieties intended for canning and storing are sown late in spring. It is particularly advantageous to grow carrots on raised beds that provide a sufficiently thick layer of loose soil. The part of the plant above ground is 20 to 30 cm tall.

Late varieties of carrot are harvested by lifting them carefully with a fork and then pulling them up by the leafy tops so as not to damage the roots.

Early carrot

Parsley

Petroselinum crispum

Parsley is native to the Mediterranean region and grows wild in the mountain regions of Europe to this day. The plant contains essential oils and a glycoside which has a diuretic effect. It is an officially recognised medicinal herb. Its pungent flavour is more delicate than that of its close relative, the parsnip. All parts are used: the root, leaves, and seeds. The seeds are used ground for seasoning foods. There are two forms - the root form and the curled leaf form, both are biennial.

Root or Hamburg parsley

Root or Hamburg parsley (*Petroselinum crispum* var. *radicosum*) is cultivated mainly for its slender, spindle-shaped, white root with a delicate aromatic flavour; the smooth leaves are also used for flavouring foods. They contain a large amount of vitamin C.

Parsley (*Petroselinum crispum* var. *vulgare*) is grown solely for its leaves. The highly curled leaves are

The very small seeds of parsley are usually pelleted so they have a rounded shape; they are often sown in wide belts instead of rows.

Parsley leaf

a kitchen herb used as a flavouring and garnish. The plants put out leaves very early in spring of the second year. The chopped leaves of both forms are also frozen for winter use.

Cultivation and harvesting

Parsley is always sown directly in open ground very early in spring (February-March), because germination is slow. It may also be sown in autumn. The plants are thinned to 10 to 20 cm apart. In shallow, compact, dry or stony soils the roots fork and become deformed. Root varieties grown for storing are not harvested until late autumn. During the summer the young roots are harvested, which are used in soups. Leaf varieties are harvested throughout the growing season. If given protective cover, the leafy forms may be harvested even in winter because parsley overwinters well. In early spring, weak roots can be put in a flowerpot or other container by a window and the leafy tops snipped as they grow.

It is interesting to note that root parsley is widely grown in Central Europe and parsnip is less popular there, whereas the people of Western Europe prefer parsnip.

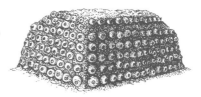

Roots are stored sandwich-fashion in mounds in the cellar or in a storage pit, but they may also be left out in the bed for the winter.

Celeriac

Apium graveolens var. *rapaceum*

Celeriac, or root celery, is a popular vegetable mainly in Central, Northern and Eastern Europe, where celery is hardly ever grown. The aromatically flavoured swollen 'bulbs' at the stem base are eaten raw or cooked as well as canned. They can be stored the whole winter.

The bulbs are crowned by broad leaf stalks and have wiry roots at the base. Good-quality celeriac should be smooth, white inside, and without any cavities. The leaves reach a height of 30 to 40 cm.

Cultivation

Celeriac is the only root vegetable that must be raised in a protected environment, for its seeds are very small and initial growth is extremely slow. The seeds are sown early in spring (February-March) into a box and the seedlings are then pricked out into modules. Seedlings are susceptible to damage by frost and should therefore not be put out until after the spring frosts. Plants are set out 30 to 50 cm apart so the leaf bud in the 'heart' of the plant is not covered with soil. Longer spells of cold weather may cause the young plants to bolt already during the first year.

The plants have deep roots and must have humus-rich, nourishing soil and an adequate, regular supply of moisture. Fresh organic manure and too much nitrogen fertiliser, however, reduce their keeping quality and result in the development of large, hollow bulbs. The oldest prostrate outer leaves may be removed at the end of summer.

Mulching the soil between individual plants with organic matter, in this case straw, is very good for celeriac. The layer of mulch retains moisture, keeps down weeds, and releases nutrients as it decomposes.

Harvesting and storing

Mature plants will tolerate a light frost but must be harvested before the onset of more severe frosts. The young leaves in the centre are left on the bulbous stems that are to be stored.

Bulbous stems that are not fully grown are harvested in summer. The variety *Apium graveolens* var. *secalinum* with delicate, aromatic leaves is sometimes grown for its foliage; in winter it can be readily grown indoors in a pot by a window.

Young celeriac plant in a block

Bulbous stem of celeriac prepared for storing

30
50

Parsnip

Pastinaca sativa

Parsnip is of Eurasian origin and in present-day Europe there is a related wild species with which it interbreeds. The plant has no special requirements. On shallow, dry, or poor soils, however, it produces smaller roots. Parsnip is hardy and very frost-resistant. It overwinters in open ground.

Parsnip gives better yields and is more reliable in cultivation than the similar root parsley. Its strongly aromatic roots are larger than the slender roots of parsley. They are also yellowish, not white, and have a sweetish flavour reminiscent of both carrot and root parsley. It contains large amounts of proteins and is therefore of great nutritional value; further important components are vitamin C and an essential oil that gives the plant its characteristic aroma. The foliage is also more vigorous, reaching a height of 40 to 50 cm. Parsnip and root parsley serve as substitutes for each other in different regions: parsnip is more popular in Western Europe, in Central Europe the more delicate and tender parsley is preferred, even though it is more demanding. Parsnip is also used in the same ways as root parsley, generally together with carrot and celeriac in cooking or as a component of dried mixed vegetables. The foliage is not used.

The roots of parsnip keep very well. In a storage pit or cellar they will keep for a long time, as long as they are not allowed to dry out. They may be covered with straw or leaves and left to overwinter in open ground, however, to be harvested in spring.

Cultivation

Parsnip is sown early in spring. Like other plants of the carrot family it germinates very slowly and its initial growth is slow. For this reason it is advisable to sow it together with a quick-maturing vegetable such as small radish in a mixed crop. The viability of parsnip seeds is short - they remain viable for only two years. The

Parsnip

seedlings should be thinned to 15 to
25 cm apart by nipping off unwanted
seedlings so that those remaining have
sufficient light for further development.

Harvesting

Parsnip may be harvested during
the summer even if it is not fully grown,
the same as celeriac, parsley, and
carrot. If it is to be stored., however, it is
among the last vegetables to be
harvested in autumn because it
tolerates frost. An earlier harvest may
be obtained by raising the plants in
a module.

Radish

Raphanus sativus var. *niger*

Radish is one of the oldest cultivated plants. It forms round, turnip- shaped, or cylindrical roots coloured white, red, purple, or black. The roots have a peppery flavour that is caused by mustard oil, which is known for its various beneficial effects on digestion. The roots are also rich in vitamin B and C. They are generally eaten raw but also cooked.

Radish is a cold-loving plant and therefore sown early in spring or late summer for autumn harvesting. It differs from small radish, in that it is larger and more vigorous (the foliage reaches a height of 20 to 30 cm), has a longer growing period, and is less prone to bolting. There are two types: summer radish, which is an annual, and winter radish, which is a biennial and is intended for storing. The summer radish of East Asian origin (*longipinnatus* type) grows fast and forms large, delicate and tender roots. It is not sown until July, to prevent bolting. Winter radish (usually black) is sown in May, and can be harvested until late autumn. When stored, it keeps well throughout the winter.

To grow good roots, radish requires deep soil, a light situation, and sufficient distance between the individual plants. On dry or poor soils, the roots have an acrid flavour and are

 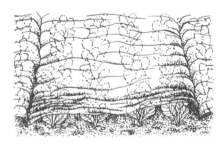

Unpleasant 'worminess' of the roots of summer radish can be avoided by growing the plants under a special thick netting (enlarged detail), which prevents the turnip fly (Chlorophila floralis) from laying eggs in the plant necks, that later develop into harmful larvae.

Japanese summer radish

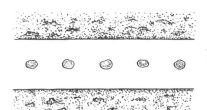

Hand sowings are generally irregular. You can, however, use seed tapes (sold in shops) to which the seeds are attached at optimum distances. There are placed in drills in the bed and covered with soil.

tough and deformed. Summer radish can be forced at low temperatures in spring and autumn in a greenhouse or polytunnel. In open ground its development and harvesting can also be speeded up by temporarily covering the plants with perforated plastic film or fibrous film.

Winter radish

15
30

Small radish

Raphanus sativus var. *radicula*

Small radishes were developed from the radish by selective breeding of small forms with short growing periods. The foliage is only 10 to 20 cm high and in very early varieties consists of only a few leaves. Small radishes from the first harvest are generally eaten raw, those harvested later are also used in cooked dishes.

Small radishes come in various shapes and colours: snow-white, rose, fiery red, purple, yellow. Especially attractive are the bicoloured varieties. Small radish has the same composition and nutritional value as radish and the same requirements, apart from the soil, which can be less deep. It is one of the quickest-maturing vegetables. Because it has such a short growing period and is a cold-loving plant, it is excellent for growing in earliest spring as well as autumn and also under various conditions - in a greenhouse, frame or polytunnel, under a floating mulch of perforated plastic film, as well as in open ground. Each of these, however, requires a suitable variety for the given conditions.

The plant's small size and rapid growth make these radishes ideal for intercropping with a slower-growing vegetable (e.g. kohlrabi or lettuce). In shaded situations and when planted thickly they do not form swollen roots. If the seeds are sown late in spring or in summer the plants bolt without forming edible roots. On dry or poor soils these radishes acquire an acrid taste and become turnip-shaped and tough. Juicy, delicately flavoured radishes can be had only if they grow no longer than

Radishes will form proper roots only if they are thinned, preferably to 5 to 6 cm apart, and the young plants thus have plenty of room and light. Radishes are thinned by nipping off unwanted plants because pulling them up would disrupt the root system of the remaining plants.

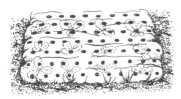

Their low habit and resistance to cold make small radishes highly suitable for speeding up their growth and harvesting by covering them with perforated plastic or fibrous film.

Red-and-white, round type of small radish

White icicle type of small radish

3-4 weeks. Belated harvesting results in spongy, split, and woody radishes. Small radishes keep for a short time only, but if the leafy tops are removed and they are stored in a cool place they will keep for as long as 2-3 weeks.

Beetroot

Beta vulgaris var. crassa

Beetroot and Swiss chard are older forms than mangelwurzel (*B. vulgaris* subsp. *vulgaris*) and sugar beet (*B. vulgaris* subsp. *altissima*). Beetroot is valued for its concentration of sugars and organic acids. Betaine is what gives the roots their typical flavour, and anthocyanin, a glycoside pigment, is what gives the flesh its reddish-purple colour, which is particularly prized for lending visual appeal to various dishes. In good-quality varieties anthocyanin is equally distributed throughout the flesh, whereas in varieties that have not been selectively bred vascular bundles form undesirable white rings on a cross-section of the root. White and yellowish-orange varieties are grown less frequently. Beetroot is generally used cooked or pickled. Young beets are also eaten raw.

Young round beetroot

Most varieties have round or flat-topped round roots, The cylindrical form of some varieties makes it possible to slice them into attractive round sections for canning or pickling. Smaller round beets are obtained from thicker sowings. They are popular because of their delicate flavour. The foliage reaches a height of 20 to 30 cm.

Cultivation and harvesting

Beetroot is sown in rows directly in the bed and the plants are thinned to 10 to 30 cm apart. Seeds are not sown until May or June for several reasons: the sprouting seedlings are readily damaged by frost, low temperatures in the initial stage of growth may cause the plants to bolt, and smaller, younger

Cultivated varieties of the genus Beta do not form separate seeds but glomerules (left) containing 2-4 seeds. The plants sprout in clumps (centre). Modern varieties have single seeds (right) so the plants do not sprout in clumps but singly, thereby also facilitating thinning.

Cylindrical beetroot

beets less than 10 cm across have a more delicate flavour. Overgrown beets are fibrous or woody. For early harvesting the seeds may be sown in a frame or modules. Beets keep well when stored but must be lifted before the first frost.

The roots are partially above ground and should be pulled up by the leafy tops so they are not damaged and do not exude juice.

Swede

Brassica napus var. *napobrassica*

Swede, or rutabaga, as it is called in North America, is one of the oldest cultivated plants. Before potatoes were introduced and began to be cultivated in Europe, it was a very important item in man's diet. It has no special requirements, is frost-resistant, and can be grown even in mountainous regions. It gives rich yields, stores well, and has many uses, both raw and cooked. It is said that in days of war, the swede saved many people from starvation. Its great nutrional value lies primarily in its protein and sugar content; it also contains significant amounts of vitamins C and B.

The roots are turnip-shaped to bulbous with tall leafy tops; they are less regular and smaller than the similar turnip roots. If sown early and harvested late, swede may become woody. Varieties with white or purple- tinged skin (*purpurescens* type) and white flesh are of poorer quality. The best varieties are those with yellowish brown skin and yellow flesh (*rutabaga* type). Swede differs from the turnip in having bluish leaves with a waxy coating.

Mature roots keep very well in a storage pit in the garden. The pit is lined with straw and the roots arranged in a pyramid with tops pointing outward. The pile is then covered with straw and on top of that with a layer of soil. Unlike other species of root vegetables where the crown of the roots must not be damaged, in the case of swede the foliage is cut off.

Swede
(purpurescens *type*)

Rutabaga
(rutabaga *type*)

Cultivation and harvesting

Swede is sown in March-April in open ground. Alternatively, plants raised in a module are put out at a later date. The roots of swede grow at a shallow depth and are partly above the surface of the soil, which is why earth is hilled up around the plants during the growing season. Swede is pulled for use in the autumn and is among the last vegetables to be harvested because it tolerates freezing temperatures as low as -10° C.

Turnip

Brassica rapa var. *rapifera*

Turnip, like swede, is a very old cultivated plant; before potatoes came to be widely grown in Europe, it played an important role in man's diet and was also important as food for livestock, especially in periods of war and poor harvests. Compared with swede it has a lower nutrional value and its flesh is more watery.

Turnip has no special heat or soil requirements and is frost-resistant. Early varieties are all white or with reddish-purple tops, others may be purple-tinged, yellow, orange, or grey to black. The plant may be distinguished from the similar swede by the grass-green leaves without a waxy coating. Good varieties for storage are the teltowiensis types with small roots coloured yellowish orange both inside and out. The flesh has a piquant flavour.

Cultivation and harvesting

Early varieties (*majalis*) which are the most commonly grown, are quick to mature so that they need only a short part of the growing season before or after another crop. The seeds can be sown directly in their final growing position, at intervals from March till September, and the young, delicately-flavoured roots are harvested throughout the growing season before they are fully mature. They may also be grown in a frame or greenhouse. Young turnips are very tasty eaten raw in salads or pickled. Fully grown turnips

Yellow teltowiensis-type turnip

are used in cooked dishes. Their low calorie content makes them suitable for weight-loss diets. Turnips for storage are sown in late summer and the fully developed roots are harvested before the onset of winter.

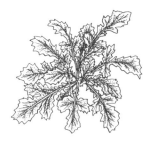

In addition to turnips grown for their roots there are also turnips that are grown for their leafy tops - these have a white root and are sown thickly for harvesting the leaves with fleshy ribs and stalks. They are used in salads or cooked. They may also be grown in a greenhouse or frame, or under plastic film.

Early turnip (majalis)

Scorzonera and salsify

Scorzonera hispanica
and *Tragopogon porrifolium*

Salsify has been cultivated since days of old but its popularity waned in favour of scorzonera (black salsify), which has greater yields and is of better quality. Both are cultivated and used in the kitchen in the same way. The roots contain inulin, making them suitable for diabetics.

Scorzonera

The roots have a high caloric as well as nutritional value. The plants are hardy but require deep, light, and nourishing soil in which they form smooth, cylindrical, black-skinned roots up to 40 cm long. The skin must either be scraped before use or else peeled after cooking. They have delicate white, almond-flavoured flesh and are eaten either raw or cooked. The foliage reaches a height of 10 to 20 cm.

The seeds are sown early in spring or in late summer. The roots may be harvested as and when required but not before they are the thickness of a pencil. Good-quality roots are firm and exude a milky liquid (latex) when broken in two. They are stored in a storage pit or cellar but it is best to leave them in the ground for the winter because they will not be damaged by frost. The roots, which flower after overwintering, retain their good quality but the flowers should be removed so they do not exhaust the plants.

Scorzonera

Salsify

The roots are yellowish, longish, cylindrical, often forked, and have an oyster-like flavour. They are not as readily damaged as scorzonera. They keep well when stored. They are frost-resistant and for that reason may even be left in the outdoor bed for the winter. However, they must be harvested before they bolt to prevent them from becoming hard and woody. The plants reach a height of 20 to 30 cm.

Scorzonera roots are brittle and break easily and must be harvested with care by lifting with a fork.

The fleshy buds of salsify are also eaten. They are harvested in spring before flowering.

Jerusalem artichoke

Helianthus tuberosus

Jerusalem artichoke is a native of South America and belongs to the same genus as sunflowers. It has become fully established in Europe as an undemanding, very hardy plant content with poor soil and harsh climates, and does well even in highland areas. It readily becomes naturalised as an escape. It tolerates shade, dry conditions and its frost-resistance makes it possible to harvest the tubers even in winter.

Most varieties have longish, irregularly knobby tubers with purple or light brown skin and white flesh. Varieties with brown tubers are cultivated more widely because they produce fewer flowers and yield a bigger crop. The tubers are 6-10 cm long and have a pronounced sweetish flavour. They are prized mainly because they contain neither starch nor saccharose but inulin and are thus a substitute for potatoes for diabetics.

Cultivation and harvesting

Jerusalem artichoke is propagated solely by means of the tubers. Best for the purpose are small tubers planted in furrows about 40 to 50 cm apart with main bud uppermost and then covered with earth. Large tubers are cut up for planting. Planting the tubers in a strip will produce a good windbreak or hedge 200 to 250 cm high. Tubers planted in spring reach maturity in September and are harvested on a cut-and-come-again

basis as required. When lifting the tubers care must be taken not to damage the skin of the tubers or the plant roots. Tubers left in the ground will

The plant stems are cut back at the end of summer to a height of about 150 cm so they will not be broken by the wind. At the end of the growing season, the foliage is cut back almost to ground level. Both the foliage and the tubers can be fed to livestock and game.

Part of a flowering plant

40 / 50

Tuber of Jerusalem artichoke

proliferate, thereby self-renewing the crop (small tubers may, of course, also become undesirable weeds of the following crop). Tubers that have been lifted from the ground soon wither and they are therefore generally stored in storage pits; it is better to leave them in the ground for the winter, however.

Potato

Solanum tuberosum

The potato, which is native to South America, was only introduced into Europe in the 16th century. Its cultivation then spread particularly during periods of war and poor harvests. Nowadays varieties are available for industrial processing (starch, alcohol, fodder), for the food industry, for immediate use, and for storage. Early varieties are eaten as a vegetable immediately after harvesting.

Some varieties form berries with seeds, others remain sterile or else simply do not flower. The tubers of most varieties have a yellowish-brown skin but rosy-skinned varieties are also grown and there are even varieties coloured bluish purple both inside and out; these are used to add variety to salads. Potatoes are nourishing and valuable because of the starch, C, A and B vitamins, and digestible proteins they contain. They are only eaten cooked. They are always stored in the dark to prevent them from turning green (which happens when they are exposed to light) which produces the poisonous alkaloid solanine. Young potatoes may also be had as a second harvest in autumn from summer planting. Only certified seed potatoes should be used for planting.

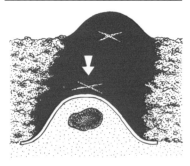

Tubers may be planted in ridges of soil covered by plastic film through cross-cuts in the film; the rows then need not be earthed up and harvesting is much earlier.

Sprouting tubers before planting

The tubers are placed in trays to sprout and in February-March they are put in a light place with a temperature below 15° C. They are planted in the bed 4-6 weeks later, when the sprouts are about 2 cm long. The distance between the plants should be 40 to 50 cm because the parts above ground are wide-branching and reach a height of 50 to 60 cm.

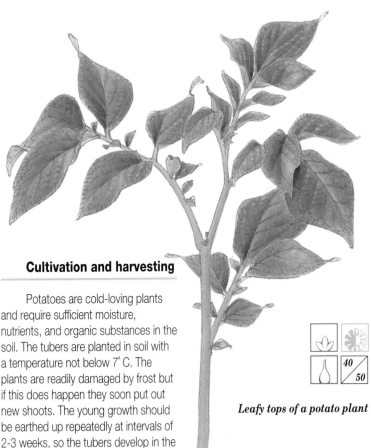

Cultivation and harvesting

Potatoes are cold-loving plants and require sufficient moisture, nutrients, and organic substances in the soil. The tubers are planted in soil with a temperature not below 7° C. The plants are readily damaged by frost but if this does happen they soon put out new shoots. The young growth should be earthed up repeatedly at intervals of 2-3 weeks, so the tubers develop in the dark. Potatoes can be harvested earlier by sprouting the tubers before planting or else by growing them in open ground under perforated plastic film at first. Early varieties are harvested during the flowering period or when the foliage begins to turn yellow. Harvesting may start by pulling away the earth and lifting developed tubers as and when potatoes are wanted or else it may be done by digging up the entire crop at once. After potatoes are harvested, the bed may be used for a further crop of vegetables, e.g. Chinese cabbage or spinach.

Leafy tops of a potato plant

Potato tuber that has sprouted

Fruiting vegetables

These vegetables are grown for their fruits. They include primarily plants of the nightshade family (Solanaceae) - tomatoes, sweet peppers, aubergines, Peruvian winter cherry, and of the gourd family (Cucurbitaceae) - marrow, melon, cucumber, as well as okra of the mallow family (Malvaceae) and artichoke of the composite family (Asteraceae). The fruits are generally eaten raw. Some, especially peppers and tomatoes, are an important source of vitamins.

The most typical characteristic of fruiting vegetables is that they are warmth-loving plants: they require a sunny situation, temperatures below 10° C halt their development and they are destroyed by frost. Growing in open ground can be supplemented by growing them under glass or plastic film, by mulching, by fencing them in with stakes and plastic film as protection against cold, or by covering them with temporary polytunnels. In unfavourable regions they are grown only in greenhouses, which yields a high-quality crop. To give the plants a sufficiently long growing period and to protect them in the initial stage of growth, they are raised in a protected environment before being put out in their final growing position - the seeds are sown in a box and the seedlings pricked out into blocks, modules, or larger flowerpots.

The plants have demanding food and moisture requirements. They must be watered regularly and it is also advisable to give them supplementary feed as they grow; they must not be

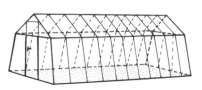

Small greenhouse

given too much nitrogen, however. Sideshoots must be removed regularly to keep foliage within bounds and the main growing point removed as required to promote the ripening of a limited number of fruits. These measures are required by cucumbers, tomatoes, and melons, especially when they are grown in a greenhouse. Fruiting vegetables can also be grown in containers, individual plastic sacks, or grow bags (large plastic bags filled with substrate, laid flat, and provided with openings on top for the plants). Good pollination must be provided for most plants of the gourd family.

The fruits must be harvested regularly as they are produced. In the case of cucumbers and courgettes, long intervals between harvesting bring the formation of further fruits to a stop.

In the case of tomatoes, aubergines, and melons the fruits become overripe. Immature fruits picked before the end of the growing season ripen well afterwards, however.

Melon mulched with plastic film

Cucumber seedling raised in a peat pot (Jiffy pot)

Truss of tomatoes tied to a cane

Tomato

Lycopersicon esculentum

Tomatoes will grow even in uncongenial conditions but for good and early fruiting they require sunlight, warmth and sufficient water. In the greenhouse they are grown only as cordons (up to 200 cm high) that require the removal of all sideshoots growing from the axils of the leaves and that have to be tied to a support. In addition to these, bush tomatoes are also grown in open ground. These are very early and are planted closer together, spaced 50 x 50 cm. Tomatoes can also be successfully grown on a balcony in containers or in grow bags. For this purpose, varieties only 40 cm high have been developed by selective breeding. Early fruiting may be promoted by covering the soil with clingfilm.

Cultivation

Tomatoes are always raised in a protected environment before being planted outside. The seedlings need to be raised in larger flowerpots or blocks (9 cm in diameter). Before being put outside, they must be well-developed and hardened off. They are put in the soil at a slant and covered with earth up to the first leaves; if they are too tall, the earth may be drawn up even higher.

For raising the plants takes a full 6 weeks. The fruits colour very well on the plant even under cover of the leaves. Strong sunlight may cause sun scorch. In August the growing points are pinched out, so the plants do not become exhausted by setting new fruits. The fruits are harvested before

The plants set fruit only after being pollinated. In greenhouses where there are insufficient air currents, self-pollination must be aided by shaking the flowers, for instance with a stick.

Pear-shaped yellow tomato

Tomatoes welcome any protection from unfavourable weather, e.g. fencing-in with stakes and plastic film. Plastic film also serves to protect the plants against damage by autumn frosts.

the frost and left to ripen in a warm place or on the cut- off plants.

Diversity of varieties

Tomatoes vary greatly both in shape and colour. The smallest varieties are the currant- , cherry- , and pear-shaped types, which are decorative and tasty. The commonest varieties are the round, medium-large tomatoes. Large, fleshy tomatoes, popular for salads, are late varieties. There are also angular, flat, and prominently ribbed types. Most productive are the F1 hybrids.

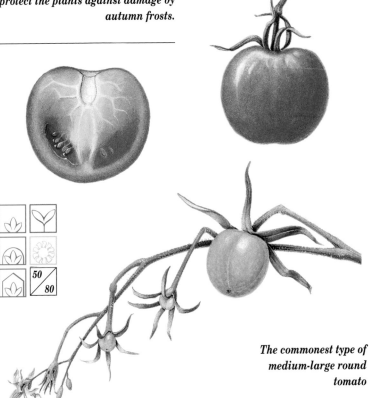

The commonest type of medium-large round tomato

Sweet pepper

Capsicum annuum

Sweet pepper has been known in Europe since the days of Christopher Columbus but has been grown as a vegetable for less than a hundred years. Of all vegetables, its fruit has the greatest concentration of vitamin C. The fruit is glossy, upright or drooping, and 2-20 cm long. The forms used as a vegetable are eaten raw, cooked or canned. The forms used as a condiment are dried and ground for seasoning. Ornamental forms with tiny fruits are grown as house plants. The hot burning sensation of some fruits is caused by the alkaloid capsaicin, also used in the pharmaceutical industry. The hottest parts of the fruit are the seeds and the partitions.

Fruit of sweet pepper gathered when fully ripe

Tomato-shaped sweet pepper

Cultivation

Sweet pepper is grown in open ground only in southern latitudes. It requires sunlight and sufficient moisture, it does not tolerate temperatures of less than 10° C, and is destroyed by frost. It has a long growing season and must therefore be sown very early in spring (February-March) and raised in flowerpots, blocks or modules. Seedlings are put out when they already have flowers and are tied to short stakes for support. The plants reach a height of 30 to 80 cm.

Harvesting

The fruits are generally gathered unripe, when they are green or yellow; they must be fully grown, however, otherwise they taste like grass. Fruits gathered when fully ripe are red, yellow, orange, or purple to violet and are usually canned. Fully ripe fruits have a distinctive flavour and the greatest nutritional value.

Vegetable varieties have an angular, conical, long pointed or tomato- like shape. Most highly prized is the thick skin of the fruit. They are generally sweet, the most popular type in Northern and Western Europe. Hot peppers are grown chiefly in Southern Europe.

Planting in a grow bag filled with a substrate makes it possible to grow plants without the use of beds. Sweet pepper also does well in containers at least 21 cm in diameter.

The best place for growing sweet pepper is in a greenhouse. Covering the soil or fencing the plants in with plastic film is also suitable.

Flowers and section of the fruit of sweet pepper

Aubergine

Solanum melongena

Aubergine is probably native to India. It is also called eggplant after the smooth egg-shaped fruits usually coloured dark greyish or blackish purple, but some varieties are coloured white or yellowish. The fleshy fruits with small seeds are eaten only cooked, usually together with other fruiting vegetables.

Cultivation

Aubergine can be grown in open ground only in southern latitudes or in sheltered situations because temperatures below 15° C stop its growth and it is destroyed by frost. In cooler regions, it is grown only in greenhouses, or else fenced in with stakes and plastic film. This protects it from low temperatures, wind and rain. Seedlings are planted 40 to 50 cm apart. They require plenty of light and regular watering to prevent them from shedding their leaves and flower buds. It is advisable to use the tried and tested method of covering the soil with plastic film or planting the plants in a grow bag like sweet peppers.

Branching can be encouraged by nipping off the central growing point. It is recommended to tie the plants to short stakes (they grow to a height of 50 to 60 cm). The glossy, dark violet to purple fruits are highly decorative. White fruits are egg-shaped, dark ones drop-shaped, oblong or cylindrical, up to 30 cm long.

Long, cylindrical fruit

A sufficiently long growing season is ensured by sowing the seeds very early (in February-March) in a greenhouse and raising the seedlings in modules or flowerpots.

Harvesting

Harvesting mature fruits encourages the growth of further fruits. To obtain fruits of a reasonable size, no more than 5 to 6 should be allowed to mature on the plant. They will keep for ten days at the most. The fruits are harvested by cutting them off when they are their typical size, glossy, and beginning to soften. Overripe fruits that are no longer glossy turn bitter.

Drop-shaped fruit

White egg-shaped aubergine

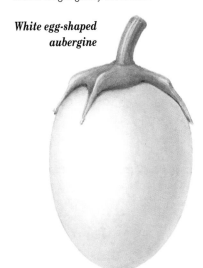

Cucumber

Cucumis sativus

The cucumber grows fast, has a shallow root system, and is sensitive to fluctuations in temperature and moisture. It requires warmth and a soil rich in organic matter. Its growth is stopped by temperatures below 10° C and it is destroyed by frost. In congenial conditions it does well even in open ground, in cooler areas it is advisable to cover the soil with plastic film or to cover the plants temporarily with a polytunnel. In less congenial conditions, good- quality fruits may be obtained only in a greenhouse. The plant trails over the ground or climbs over a trellis.

Cultivation

Cucumbers are divided into two groups according to how they are used: gherkins with small fruits are used for pickling; cucumbers are cultivated as a garden vegetable and eaten raw. Gherkins are generally grown outside; cucumbers are grown under various conditions and the variety must be chosen accordingly. The plants reach a length of 150 to 250 cm and the distance between them should be 40 to 60 cm. Under glass or plastic film they are grown on a supporting framework and greenhouse types must be pruned.

Cucumbers for greenhouse cultivation are always grown from plants raised in a protected environment. Seedlings can also be grown in grow bags on a ledge.

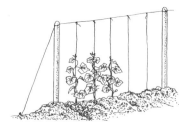

Gherkins grown in open ground were formerly allowed to trail over the ground, like cucumbers. Training on wires, however, protects them from disease.

Outdoor cucumber

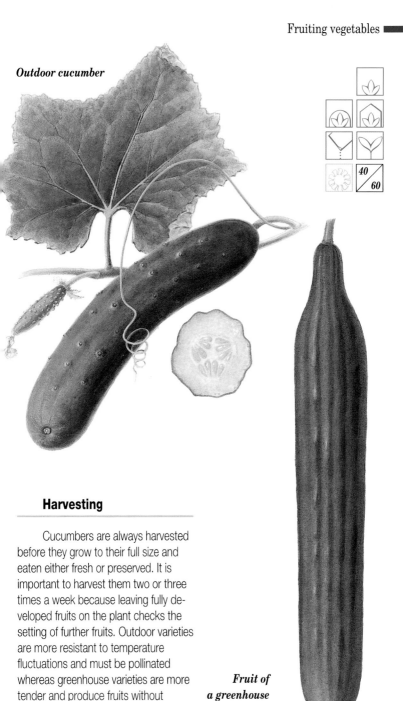

Harvesting

Cucumbers are always harvested before they grow to their full size and eaten either fresh or preserved. It is important to harvest them two or three times a week because leaving fully developed fruits on the plant checks the setting of further fruits. Outdoor varieties are more resistant to temperature fluctuations and must be pollinated whereas greenhouse varieties are more tender and produce fruits without fertilisation.

Fruit of a greenhouse cucumber

Marrow and Pumpkin

Cucurbita pepo and *Cucurbita maxima*

Marrows are the largest and fastest-growing vegetables and are marked by an amazing variety. They require an adequate supply of water and an abundant supply of nutrients, humus-rich soil, and lots of sun. The plants are destroyed by even a light frost. The fruits are eaten cooked or pickled. The large oily seeds are a favourite snack in some countries.

Marrow

Marrow, which does well even in less congenial conditions, includes chiefly small bush varieties whose fruits are harvested when they are young and immature (courgettes, zucchini, custard marrows). This species furthermore includes varieties whose fruits are harvested when fully ripe, primarily spaghetti marrow, oil marrow (var. *oleifera*) with skinless seeds, and ornamental gourds. Trailing varieties can be trained and tied to a supporting construction.

Pumpkin

Pumpkin has much greater heat requirements, forms long trailing stems and its fruits are used when fully ripe to make compotes and pie fillings. They are harvested before the first frosts and left to ripen fully afterwards. The ripe fruits may be round, loaf-shaped, pointed, or a 'turban' shape with green, white, yellowish-brown or orange skin. A single plant produces about three fully-ripe fruits weighing dozens of kilos each. Some varieties can be stored.

100/200

Pumpkin, orange variety

94

In the case of courgettes and custard marrows, harvesting of the immature fruits encourages the formation of new fruits.

The female flower (right) differs from the male flower (left) in that the embryonic fruit is visible beneath the petals. In an enclosed environment and in poor weather, setting fruit must be assisted by hand pollination.

Cultivation

The development of marrows and pumpkins can be speeded up by raising seedlings in flowerpots or modules, by mulching the soil with plastic film or by covering the seedlings with polytunnels. Because of their large size marrows and pumpkins should be well-fed before being planted . They also do well in soil that has been fertilised in the autumn with fresh manure and extremely well when grown directly on compost. Marrows are planted approximately 60 cm apart, pumpkins 100 to 200 cm apart.

Courgette

Okra

Hibiscus esculentus

Okra, or gumbo, is in all probability native to India or Africa and was already known in Egypt in the second millennium BC but is not widely grown - it is grown only in tropical and subtropical areas. It is an annual, highly warmth-loving plant that requires sufficient sun; it is damaged by low temperatures and destroyed by frost. In less congenial conditions, it must be fenced in with stakes and plastic film or grown in a greenhouse.

Cultivation and harvesting

The seeds germinate only at temperatures above 15° C. It is advisable to soak the seeds for 24 hours before sowing. The plants are 50 to 100 cm high, upright, slightly branched, with decorative, palmate leaves and striking, gleaming yellow flowers with purple blotches in the centre. Branching can be promoted by nipping off the growing points.

The fruits, fleshy pods, develop continuously, reach a length of 10 to 20 cm, and contain 30 to 60 round grey seeds when ripe. They are elongated, pointed, and erect, which is why this vegetable is also called 'ladies' fingers'.

Their surface is finely grooved and velvety. Older pods are fibrous and coarse. For that reason pods are harvested young, when they are about 3 to 6 cm long, still tender and crisp, and when the seeds are just beginning to form. Fresh pods do not keep nor do they tolerate long transport. They can be stored after they have dried. They are generally green, but Syrian varieties are red.

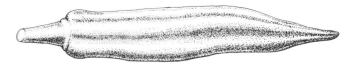

Detail and section of pod

Plant with flower and young pods

Uses

The pods are used in soups or stews or else they are canned. Generally, however, they are used in mixtures together with other fruiting vegetables - sweet peppers, tomatoes, aubergines, courgettes. They are often a component of frozen mixed vegetables to which they impart a delicate, piquant flavour. They are valued chiefly for their content of mucilaginous substances. The dried powdered mature fruits are used as a flavouring. The dried roasted seeds are sometimes used as a coffee substitute or for the extraction of oil. The green seeds are often canned like peas.

Watermelon

Citrullus vulgaris

Watermelon is a highly warmth-loving plant with spreading stems about 200 to 300 cm long, typical palmate leaves and pale yellow unisexual flowers, i.e. either male or female. Generally, it is only grown outside and therefore only in southern, sunny, sheltered areas. Its growth is halted by temperatures below 15° C and it is destroyed by frost. The plant's large root system ensures its provision with water even in dry conditions. Only very occasionally is it grown in the greenhouse, on a supporting framework. The fruits, with sweet juicy flesh, are eaten raw and stand up very well to transport. They are round, oval, pear-shaped, or in the shape of a short cylinder, and up to 40 cm long.

Cultivation

Watermelon plants are always raised in a protected environment before being put outside. In addition to the usual methods described for other fruiting vegetables, the seeds are popularly sown into blocks of turf turned upside down. The seedlings are planted 80 to 150 cm apart and it is recommended that they be temporarily covered with polytunnels. Only annual varieties with smaller fruits 15-20 cm in diameter are suitable for less congenial conditions. The main growing point should be nipped off to encourage branching and sideshoots should be shortened. When grown under cover it is necessary to hand-pollinate the flowers to assist formation of fruits, as for marrows. Warm soil is beneficial to the growth of the plants and therefore in less congenial conditions it is mulched with black plastic film that in addition

The seeds are oval, almost black, unlike those of ordinary melon, which are cream-coloured and pointed at both ends.

keeps down weeds. The ripe fruit is dark green, light green, or mottled. Mature fruits give a hollow sound when tapped and it is furthermore possible to determine if they are ripe for harvesting by the fact that dew does not condense on their surface in the morning. The fruit does not have a cavity and the seeds are scattered throughout the red or, less frequently, yellowish pulp. Some F1 hybrids have seedless fruits.

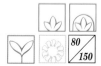

Part of a watermelon plant with fruit and section of the ripe fruit

Melon

Cucumis melo

Melon is hardier than watermelon and grown more widely. It is a trailing or climbing vine with stems 150 to 200 cm long.

Cultivation

In warmer areas it can be grown outside. In less congenial areas, the plants must be protected temporarily by fencing them in with stakes and plastic film or by covering them with polytunnels. They are damaged by temperatures below 10° C and destroyed by frost. In cooler climates, they may be grown only in greenhouses. Only early varieties are grown and the plants are always trained on a supporting framework to which the fruits are tied. Seedlings are always raised in a protected environment before being put out in order to extend the growing period. The flowers are usually male or female. In a protected place which does not allow the access of insects, the flowers must be hand pollinated, the same as for marrows. The main growing point in young plants should be nipped off. The sideshoots should also be pinched out, leaving only one fruit on each.

Section of the fruit of a musk melon

Part of a flowering plant

Fruit shapes

Melon plants respond very well to mulching of the soil with plastic film. Their early cropping as well as their hardiness can be improved by grafting on marrow stock.

The fruits have a central cavity filled with seeds. The flesh is generally orange but may also be creamy or greenish, with a pronounced musky odour when ripe. The fruits are generally round, often elongated to long, snake-like shapes. They are eaten raw or frozen.

The major types are cantaloupe melons with rough, ridged skin, musk melons with corky netted skin, and winter or casaba melons with smooth yellow skin. Casaba melons can be stored whereas the other types readily become overripe and tend to spoil during transport.

Sweet corn

Zea mays var. saccharata

Sweet corn is one of the oldest cultivated plants. It is native to South America, is classed among the grasses and is grown for its kernels that form a fruiting spike or ear.

Cultivation

Sweet corn is a warmth-loving plant; its growth is halted by low temperatures and it is destroyed by frost. It can, of course, be grown even in less congenial areas by choosing an early variety, a suitable site, and sowing the seeds in warm soil with a temperature of at least 12° C. The plant's development can be greatly speeded up by sowing the seeds or planting seedlings raised in a protected environment through transparent or black plastic film mulch that raises the soil temperature and retains the soil moisture as well as preserving its structure. In cooler climates, seedlings are protected by fencing them in with stakes and plastic film or by covering them with perforated plastic film or growing them under cloches. To increase the stability of the plants, which are 80 to 120 cm high, it is recommended to earth up the stems.

Harvesting

Sweet corn is harvested when the kernels are full but immature. The best time, when the kernels are at their most nutritious, can be determined by pressing a fingernail into a kernel. If the liquid that appears is not watery and the

Corn with plastic film mulch

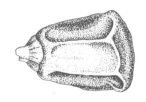

Unlike feed corn, the kernels of sweet corn have a high sugar content. When they are fully ripe this manifests itself by their becoming wrinkled and angular. There are also new 'supersweet' varieties.

Ear ripe for harvesting

kernel still gives under pressure, then the cob is ripe for picking. Cobs should be consumed as soon as they are picked because they rapidly lose their food value. Very young cobs, barely 10 cm long, can be canned or pickled whole. Generally, however, the semisoft kernels are first scraped from the cobs and then cooked, canned, or frozen.

50 / 60

Part of plant with flowering spike (ear) enclosed by bracts

Globe artichoke

Cynara scolymus

Globe artichokes are vigorous, highly branched, thistle-like perennial plants, 120 to 140 cm high, with large decorative, bluish-purple flowers and compound leaves. They are grown for the flower buds which have an edible fleshy bottom at the base of the outer scales and top of the flower stem. The buds are harvested with a short stem when they are fully developed and measure 8-10 cm across but are as yet unopened.

Cultivation

Globe artichokes have been grown in southern latitudes for several thousands of years. They are destroyed by more severe frosts but tolerate low temperatures above freezing point fairly well. In more northern latitudes, the underground parts of the plant survive the winter but only if provided with suitable protection. In less congenial conditions, the hardier French varieties are more successful than the more demanding Italian varieties.

They need fertile, nourishing soil and watering. They produce numerous offshoots but only two main shoots should be left on the plant for proper development of the flower buds. The edible parts - young flower buds or

Flower bud ready for harvesting

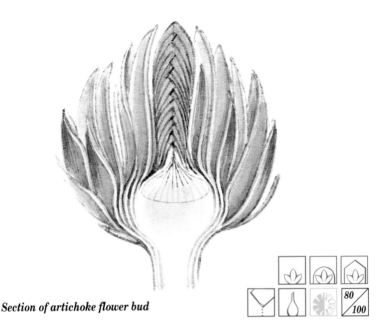

Section of artichoke flower bud

fleshy bottoms - are generally eaten cooked with a sauce, canned, or pickled; they can also be eaten raw, however. They are very delicate and tasty.

Harvesting

All the flower buds must be harvested before the first frost. Stems with buds that are not fully developed can be cut off before winter and heeled in in sand where they will grow to the required extent. In Central Europe, the parts above ground are cut off before the winter and the remainder of the plants covered with bracken, straw, or leaves, possibly also with soil. Even dug-up plants can overwinter in a frame or cellar. Plants are left in place for four years at the most.

Globe artichokes can be readily propagated from seed sown early in spring. Cultivated varieties, however, are better grown by vegetative propagation from rooted offsets to ensure uniformity and quality.

Peruvian winter cherry

Physalis peruviana

All members of this genus are notable for their dry inflated calyxes with united sepals enclosing the fruit - a round, juicy berry. Peruvian winter cherry is less well known than the closely related perennial Chinese lantern (*Physalis alkekengi*), whose gleaming red-orange 'lanterns' are a decorative feature of the garden or in a vase throughout the winter. Unlike ornamental species, the plants of Peruvian winter cherry are smaller, more highly branched, and the calyxes are yellow-green. The berries inside, however, are larger, about the size of a cherry, and edible. They have a sweetish-sour flavour and a pleasant pineapple-like aroma; furthermore they contain healthy pectins.

Cultivation

Peruvian winter cherry does well in warmer areas and sunny sites. Otherwise it has no special requirements. Seedlings are raised in a protected environment (from March) and after the spring frosts are planted 40 to 50 cm apart with the first flower buds already set. They respond very well to plastic film mulches and produce larger crops in polytunnels, in a plastic greenhouse or when fenced in at least temporarily with stakes and plastic film. It is advisable to tie them to stakes so the plants do not topple over.

Harvesting and uses

The flowers are yellowish green. The sepals unite and enclose berries that are almost spherical, an

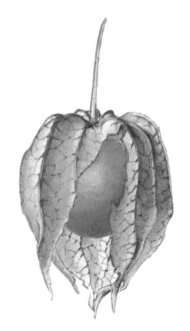

Ripe fruit enclosed by the membranous calyx

inconspicuous yellow-orange colour when ripe, and filled with small seeds. After removing the calyx, they are eaten raw, stewed, candied, made into jam or jelly, or dried. They are dried in the sun or drying shed and are somewhat like raisins. The fruits together with the calyx are harvested as they are produced as they ripen from August until the first frosts, that 'burn' the plants. The calyxes are not separated from the berries until they are to be used.

Peruvian winter cherry plant
with developing fruits

Legumes

Legumes are a numerically small, uniform. group because they belong to a single family, namely the pea family (Fabaceae). The flowers are papilionaceous, the fruits seed pods, and there are nodules on the roots. The symbiotic bacteria inhabiting these nodules, visible with the naked eye, are capable of binding atmospheric nitrogen. The plants thus obtain the nitrogen they need in a way that is unique among the vegetables. They do not require the application of nitrogen fertiliser and enrich the soil with nitrogen for following crops. Formation of the nodules can be stimulated by inoculating the seeds with bacterial preparations specific for the given species.

Members of this family are among the oldest cultivated plants. Because of the high protein content of the seeds they, along with cereal grasses, were of prime importance in man's diet already in days of old. Chickpeas, soy beans, peanuts, broad beans and other beans and peas were grown solely for the edible seeds. Some species, chiefly peas, broad and other beans, gradually began to be grown as vegetables eaten young before they are fully ripe. Either the whole pods or the immature shelled seeds are eaten. They are also popular canned, frozen, and dried.

Peas clinging to netting by means of tendrils

Cultivation

Legumes have moderate requirements as to soil fertility. They should be rotated with other crops. They require a sheltered site and timely removal of weeds. Some species are very hardy, particularly peas and broad beans; other beans, however, are all warmth-loving plants and do not tolerate frost. Shops usually offer treated seeds so that in cold soils they

Climbing French bean

are not destroyed by parasitic micro-organisms. They are generally sown directly outside and are often pregerminated before sowing. It is recommended that warmth-loving species be protected by plastic film or cloches while germinating.

Legumes are self-pollinating but for good pollination they require a suitable temperature, i.e. not too high. Bush varieties grow upright, whereas climbing varieties require a support to which the plants cling by means of tendrils or by twining.

Habit of a dwarf bush French bean

Garden peas

Pisum sativum

Peas are among the oldest cultivated plants, found already in excavations of ancient Troy. Originally they were grown for the ripe dry, edible seeds. Immature seeds did not begin to be used until the 17th century by the Dutch. This gave rise to the garden pea, which has a high calorie content and is rich in vitamins.

Wrinkled pea

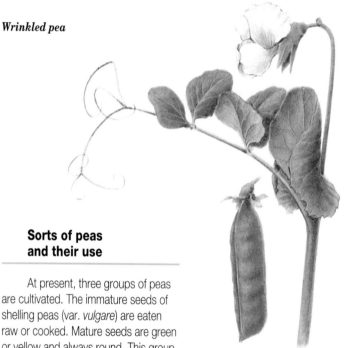

Sorts of peas and their use

At present, three groups of peas are cultivated. The immature seeds of shelling peas (var. *vulgare*) are eaten raw or cooked. Mature seeds are green or yellow and always round. This group best tolerates low temperatures but the seeds soon become overripe and less sweet and tender.

Commonest are the fleshy wrinkled peas (var. *medullare*) that are excellent for canning, freezing as well as drying. They are readily affected by low temperatures and are therefore sown later than other peas. They remain tender and retain their sweet flavour longer. Least common are sugar peas (var. *saccharatum*), of which the pods are eaten. These very tender pods do not form the interior membrane other peas have. The young pods are harvested. These are eaten whole, unshelled, raw or cooked. Their seeds are not suited for cooking because they remain tough and are less tasty. Crisp types of sugar pea have thick-walled pods. Sugar peas tolerate even lower temperatures than other peas. The pods of all mangetout peas are harvested as they are produced before they become overripe.

Semi-leafless self-supporting peas are a newly developed type with limited leaf surface. Photosynthesis and mutual support are provided by highly branched tendrils.

Seeds should be soaked in lukewarm water to swell before sowing and should be sown 25 to 35 cm apart.

Pod of sugar pea

Tall and moderately tall types of peas require a support to which the plants cling with tendrils. The simplest way is to drive stakes into the ground among the plants; you can also use wire mesh or netting.

Wrinkled peas have sweet seeds; they contain simple sugars instead of starch and the surface of mature seeds is markedly wrinkled.

Beans

Phaseolus sp.

Beans are climbing or bush plants grown as annuals. Vegetable varieties are grown primarily for the unripe pods but the dry, ripe seeds may also be used. The unripe seeds of all beans must be cooked before eating in order to destroy the toxins they contain.

Scarlet runner beans

Phaseolus coccineus

These are hardier than French beans and are cross-pollinated. The flat, fleshy pods, up to 30 cm long, are harvested until the first frosts. The older pods of some varieties have strings that must be removed before cooking. The seeds are the largest of all beans and are used at all stages of their development. The ripe seeds of scarlet runner beans are great favourites because of their size and excellent flavour. For forcing in tall greenhouses, particularly tender, stringless varieties with white flowers and white seeds were developed. The original forms have bicoloured red-and-white flowers and are often grown for ornament. The pods are markedly rough and pointed, the seeds flat kidney-shaped.

French beans

Phaseolus vulgaris

French beans are the beans most widely grown. There are two forms: one climbing 250 to 300 cm high and the dwarf bush type, which is only 30 to 40 cm high. They require a warm and sheltered site. During germination the plants may be damaged by temperatures of 1-2° C and therefore

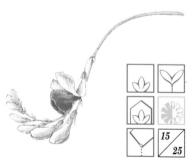

Bicoloured red-and-white inflorescence of scarlet runner beans

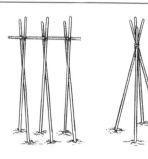

Frameworks for climbing beans

the seeds are treated and sown only after the soil has warmed.

Dwarf bush varieties are sown in rows 10 to 20 cm apart; they are early and heavy croppers and can be sown in batches until the beginning of July. Harvesting the pods promotes the growth of new ones. Yellowish green varieties, called wax beans, are especially tender.

Climbing varieties require a supporting framework. They cling by twining round the support, preferably round poles at least 2.5 m high. The seeds are station sown around the support. The pods vary in shape as well as colour and may even be mottled or almost black. The ripe seeds likewise vary markedly in shape.

The pods of both types of new varieties are stringless and without a membrane and are harvested while still crisp. The dry, mature seeds are eaten cooked.

Mature mottled pod and seed of climbing French bean

Dwarf bush French bean

Broad bean

Faba vulgaris var. *major*

Broad beans were among the first cultivated
plants. Originally only the flour from the dried seeds
was used. Nowadays, forms with smaller seeds are
grown for feed and other types (var. *major*) are eaten
as a vegetable, mainly the immature seeds that have
a high protein content. They have a delicately bitter
flavour; more recent varieties are sweet.

Broad bean plants are up to
100 cm high and have an angular stem
with little branching. The papilionaceous
flowers are bicoloured - white with
reddish-brown blotches on the wings.
The pods are about 10 cm long,
rounded, and fleshy. Only very young
beans are eaten whole, otherwise the
seeds are extracted from developed
unripe pods and then used either
cooked in various dishes, canned (this
form is very popular) or frozen. Ripe dry
seeds from the blackened, leathery
pods can be cooked for eating in
winter.

*The seed of broad beans is large
and has an irregularly flat shape.
It is coloured green, light yellowish
brown, brown, or pink.*

Cultivation

The plants tolerate cold weather
and are therefore grown also in northern
latitudes, where they even flower earlier.
Germinating plants tolerate
temperatures as low as -5° C. In mild
winters, seedlings are capable of
overwintering if provided with suitable
cover. Only some varieties do well at
higher temperatures.

Broad beans require good soil
and sufficient moisture to prevent them
from shedding their flowers. Watering
also reduces the danger of attack by
pests. The growth of nitrogen-fixing
bacteria may be encouraged by
inoculating the seeds with a special
preparation. Generally, seeds are sold
that have been treated to increase their
resistance to infection in cold soil during
germination. If the seeds have not been
treated, they should be soaked in
lukewarm water for several hours before
sowing so they germinate more quickly.
It is recommended to hill the soil around
the plants before flowering. Plants of
varieties with taller growth should be

Flowering broad bean plant

Pods ripe for harvesting

provided with a support of horizontally stretched wires attached to poles; small branches driven into the ground will suffice for plants of lower growth. Nipping off the growing point when the plants are in full flower will promote the growth of the pods and suppress infestation by aphids.

Onions and related vegetables

All these plants belong to the lily family (Liliaceae). They are divided into two groups: species with true, highly developed bulbs that die back at the end of the growing season, e.g. common onion, shallot, garlic, and species with less-developed bulbs that do not die back, e.g. chives, leek.

Cultivation

These vegetables have different requirements. Those of the first group require sufficient water in the early stages; mature bulbs, however, require dry conditions to die back. If they are grown for storage, they must not be given too much nitrogenous fertiliser. Species grown for their foliage, on the other hand, tolerate even fresh organic manuring. Onions require fertile soil, open, well-ventilated sites, and rotation of crops so they are not affected by disease. They are all frost-resistant and can be sown as well as planted even in the autumn for overwintering. The seeds may be sown directly outside but the plants are generally raised in a protected environment first. Some are propagated by division of the clumps (e.g. chives, shallots) or by planting segments of the bulbs (garlic).

The development of the edible parts depends on the temperature and day length and for that reason it is recommended to grow tried-and-tested varieties for the given district.

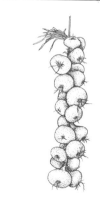

Onion bulbs plaited for storing

Flowerpot with forced foliage of onion, celery, and parsley

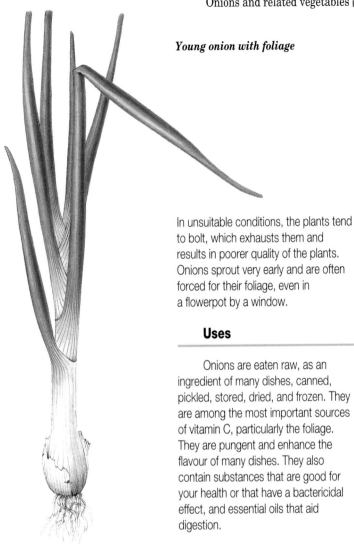

Young onion with foliage

In unsuitable conditions, the plants tend to bolt, which exhausts them and results in poorer quality of the plants. Onions sprout very early and are often forced for their foliage, even in a flowerpot by a window.

Uses

Onions are eaten raw, as an ingredient of many dishes, canned, pickled, stored, dried, and frozen. They are among the most important sources of vitamin C, particularly the foliage. They are pungent and enhance the flavour of many dishes. They also contain substances that are good for your health or that have a bactericidal effect, and essential oils that aid digestion.

Sets are small bulbs specially grown by sowing thickly and harvested the previous year. In spring they are planted so that the tips protrude just above the soil. Sets must not be more than 2 cm wide, otherwise the plants bolt.

Common onion and Shallots

Allium cepa and *Allium ascalonicum*

Both species are a rich source of vitamin C throughout the year. They contain substances with a bactericidal and fungicidal effect as well as substances that reduce swelling. The mix of essential oils gives them their typical pungent onion flavour and aroma which makes onion an irreplaceable vegetable.

Common onion

In spring the whole plants are harvested, together with the leafy tops. In winter the foliage, grown in a flowerpot by the window, is highly prized; it has a far greater vitamin C content than the bulb. Small bulbs are pickled. White varieties that do not keep well are less pungent and are eaten raw.

The earliest harvest is from spring plantings of sets or from later summer sowing of overwintering varieties that tolerate freezing temperatures as low as -20° C. In the early stages of growth, the plants require sufficient moisture,

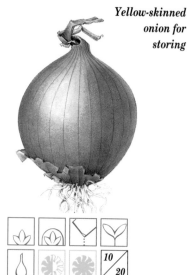

Yellow-skinned onion for storing

Seedlings from thickly sown seeds must be thinned. Autumn sowings are not thinned until spring. Carefully lifted plants can be used for planting - the roots and foliage must be cut back before doing so.

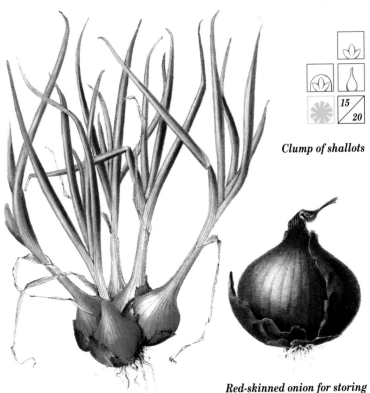

Clump of shallots

Red-skinned onion for storing

but towards the end of the growing season they require dry conditions in order to die back properly. Onions intended for storage must not be given too much nitrogen fertiliser, for that would reduce their keeping qualities. The plants should be pulled up before all the foliage dies back and they should be left lying on the bed for several days, after which they are gathered and dried. Onions must be stored in dry conditions. They tolerate temperatures below -10° C.

Shallots

Shallots resemble the common onion, but are perennial plants and the bulbs do not grow singly but in clumps; they are smaller than those of the common onion (the bulbs together with the foliage reach a height of 20 to 30 cm, whereas the common onion may be up to 50 cm tall), are spindle-shaped, and keep well - they may be stored for up to two years. A clump consists of 3-12 elongated yellow to reddish-purple bulbs that die back. Shallots have a more pungent, delicate flavour. Propagation is by means of bulbs from divided clumps planted 15 to 20 cm apart early in spring or late autumn. Both the bulbs and the delicate foliage are used. For storage, the bulbs are lifted when the foliage has toppled.

Chives and Welsh onion

Allium schoenoprasum and *A. fistulosum*

Both species are perennial plants and grown chiefly for the foliage.

Chives

Chives form frost-resistant clumps of numerous shoots 29 to 30 cm tall. They are grown solely for cutting the leaves. Their foliage is the finest of all onions and is eaten raw. Chives have no special requirements but need plenty of light and water. The leaves are snipped for use on a cut-and-come-again basis. The leaves die back in dry conditions and for the winter. Young leaves are a rich source of vitamin C, older leaves are of lesser value.

At the end of winter chives grown in a pot provide the first and most readily available greens. In the autumn the clumps are dug up, left to dry and freeze and soaked in lukewarm water before being put in a flowerpot.

Welsh onion

This is a highly frost-resistant onion grown for its foliage. In favourable conditions, it grows continuously (the foliage reaches a height of about 40 cm), in unfavourable conditions the leaves die and grow anew in spring. Either the leaves or whole plants are used. The leaves are cut for the last time two months before the temperature permanently drops below

In the fistulosum variety viviparum, the flower stems are not topped by flowers but by red bulbils up to 3 cm across often arranged in several tiers. They have a biting flavour and are used in cooking and for new planting.

The pale purple flowers of chives are decorative (they look lovely in a vase) but exhaust the plant and should be removed. Cutting the leaves delays flowering.

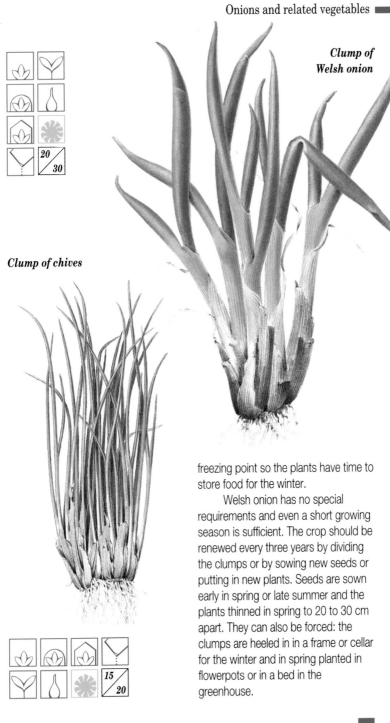

**Clump of
Welsh onion**

Clump of chives

freezing point so the plants have time to store food for the winter.

Welsh onion has no special requirements and even a short growing season is sufficient. The crop should be renewed every three years by dividing the clumps or by sowing new seeds or putting in new plants. Seeds are sown early in spring or late summer and the plants thinned in spring to 20 to 30 cm apart. They can also be forced: the clumps are heeled in in a frame or cellar for the winter and in spring planted in flowerpots or in a bed in the greenhouse.

Garlic

Allium sativum

Garlic is a steppe plant that was greatly valued for its supposedly invigorating properties as early as five thousand years ago in Egypt. Nowadays it is grown from Scandinavia to the tropics. It is widely used as a seasoning in cooking and also in pickling vegetables because it contains substances with bactericidal and fungicidal effects. It has a strong pungent flavour and aroma caused by volatile oils.

Cultivation and harvesting

Garlic is generally grown as an overwintering crop which gives larger yields, less often as a spring-planted crop. For each method there are different varieties that are suitable. To develop well, the bulb requires exposure to a temperature of 1 to 10° C for about two months. Garlic is propagated only by vegetative means because it has completely lost the ability to produce seeds. The cloves should be planted upright with the pointed tip upwards; they should not be split off from the bulb until just before planting.

On heavy soils and on freshly manured ground, garlic is susceptible to disease. It must not be grown repeatedly in the same site; the cloves must be treated in a solution of chemical preparations against root diseases and nematodes before planting. Most important, of course, is to use healthy, uninfected plants. For early harvesting, plants can be raised in a module. Plants are harvested when the leaves turn yellow, before they die back.

Garlic bulbs are best stored hanging with plaited dried leaves in a dry, well-ventilated place.

Cultivated types

One type has a compact bulb with smaller cloves and does not form a flower stalk at all. It is suitable for storage. The other type produces a tall flower stem with inflorescence enclosed

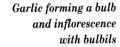

*Garlic forming a bulb
and inflorescence
with bulbils*

in a sheath. The floral organs are
rudimentary and sterile, however.
Instead of seeds, bulbils are formed in
the inflorescences that can be used for
planting. The compound bulbs of the
latter type have fewer, larger cloves.
The bulbs readily fall apart and the
flower stalk is visible in the centre. They
give larger yields, but do not keep as
well. Both types reach a height of 40 to
70 cm.

Garlic forming no flower stalk

Leek

Allium porrum

Leek is nowadays grown all over the world. It forms a large amount of matter both underground and above, and therefore requires a deep, fertile, and moisture-retentive soil.

The edible part is the thick white stem and the white bulb that does not die back. The stem is usually 10-80 cm long and is harvested together with younger leaves. Leek is frost-resistant; in areas with severe winters, so-called winter leeks with dark green, waxy leaves and short stems will do better

Putting seedlings in the outdoor bed.

The length of the white stem may be increased by planting the plants deeper and earthing them up several times during the growing season.

than summer leeks, which have pale green, upright leaves, long stems, and survive only mild winters. Pearl onions are usually considered to be a type of common onion but they are in fact a variety of leek. The small, white, tender bulbs form a cluster and are covered by a delicate skin so that they do not have to be peeled. They are used for pickling.

Leek contains essential oils whose flavour is milder than in the other onions, it is also rich in vitamin C and provitamin A, that migrate from the leaves to the stem in stored leeks. Leek retains its aromatic flavour as well as natural colour even when dried or frozen.

Cultivation

Leek is always grown from plants raised in a protected environment (seeds sown in March) because it needs a long growing season and its initial growth is slow. Before plants raised in a seedbed are put out in their final growing positions, it is necessary to shorten both the roots and the foliage so they take hold more readily. Leeks can also be 'multisown' in a module, sowing several seeds in each unit.

Harvesting

Leek is harvested late in the autumn or left in the bed, where it will remain for several months at harvest ripeness. It may be left to overwinter in the bed but it is better to dig up the plants, heel them in at an angle in a furrow in a sheltered bed, and cover the roots and white stems with soil. In a severe winter they may be covered with straw or bracken so they are not damaged by frost and are readily available whenever they are wanted. After overwintering, they must be used very early in spring before they start setting flowers and while they still are of prime quality.

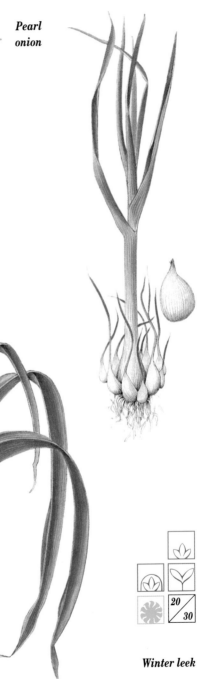

Pearl onion

Winter leek

Index

artichoke   84
asparagus   28, 52, 53
- cultivation   53
- harvesting   53
- setting out young plants   53
- shoots   52, 53
aubergine   8, 9, 84, 90, 91, 97
- cultivation   90
- harvesting   91
- sowing   91

beans   8, 108, 112
beetroot   42, 58, 59, 72, 73
- cultivation   72
- harvesting   72, 73
bolt   11, 15, 28, 30, 33, 38, 40, 45, 46, 54, 55, 64, 68, 72, 79
brassicas   7, 8, 10-29
- cultivation   10
- diseases   11
broad bean   108, 114
- cultivation   114
broccoli   10, 18, 19
- cultivation   19
- harvesting   19
- heading type   18
Brussels sprouts   8, 10, 22
- cultivation   22
- harvesting   23
bulbils   120, 123

cabbage   10, 12, 14
- cultivation   12
- harvesting   12
- storing   11, 12, 13
cabbage lettuce   30
cantaloupe melons   101
cardoon   28, 48
- blanching   48
- cultivation   48
- harvesting   48, 49
carrot   8, 58, 60, 61, 67
- cultivation   60
- fly   60, 61
- harvesting   61
- sowing   60, 61
casaba melons   101
cauliflower   8, 10, 16, 19

- cultivation   16
- harvesting   17
celeriac   58, 64, 65
- cultivation   64
- harvesting   64
- storing   64
celery   28, 29, 44, 64, 116
- blanching   44
- cultivation   44
- harvesting   44, 45
chicory   28, 29, 32, 33, 34, 35
- cultivation   32
- forcing   33
chinese cabbage   11, 26, 27, 83
- cultivation   26
- storing   26, 27
chinese mustard   40, 41
chives   116, 120, 121
- cultivation   120
- forcing   120
- harvesting   120
- sowing   120
club root   11, 20
common onion   116, 118, 119
- cultivation   118
- storing   119
compost   6, 7, 10
courgettes   94, 95
- harvesting   95
cucumber   6, 8, 9, 84, 92
- cultivation   92
- harvesting   93
custard marrows   94, 95
- harvesting   95

dandelion   36, 37
- blanching   37
- cultivation   37
- harvesting   37

endive   28, 29, 34, 35
- blanching   34
- cultivation   34
escarole   35

fertilizing   6, 7, 58, 64, 84, 108, 122
fibrous film   9, 15, 16, 18, 24, 29, 30, 69, 71
follow-on crop   9
forecrop   9
frame   8, 59, 70, 73, 76, 77, 121
French beans   109 112, 113,
- cultivation   109 112, 113,
fruiting vegetables   84-107

- cultivation   84
- harvesting   85

garden cress   8, 28, 38,
- cultivation   38
- harvesting   38
garden peas   110
- harvesting   111
garlic   116, 122, 123
- cultivation   122
- harvesting   122
globe artichoke   104, 105
- cultivation   104
- harvesting   105
glossy-leaves lettuce   30
greenhouse   8, 15, 16, 24, 26, 28, 34, 45, 69,
70, 76, 77, 84, 86, 89, 91, 92, 96, 98, 100, 121
grow bag   84, 89, 90
growing-on   8, 12, 15, 16, 17, 21, 22, 24, 26,
30, 34, 41, 45, 46, 48, 53, 64, 73, 75, 85, 86,
89, 91, 92, 95, 99, 102, 106, 124
growing period   7
gumbo   96

Hamburgh parsley   62, 63
horseradish   58, 59

Iceberg lettuce   30, 31
intercropping   23, 70

Jerusalem artichoke   58, 80, 81
- cultivation   80
- harvesting   80

kale   10, 13, 20
- cultivation   21
- harvesting   21
kohlrabi   8, 11, 19, 23, 24, 25, 70
- cultivation   24
- varieties   24, 25

'ladies' fingers'   96
lamb's lettuce   28, 36
- cultivation   36
- harvesting   36
leaf blade Swiss chard   42
leaf cabbage   20
leaf vegetables   7, 9, 28-55
- classification   28
- cultivation   29
leek   8, 29, 116, 124, 125
- cultivation   124
- harvesting   125

legumes   7, 9, 108-115
lettuce   8, 9, 19, 23, 28, 31, 32, 34, 70
- cultivation   30
- harvesting   31
long heads lettuce   31

marrow   6, 8, 9, 84, 94, 95, 99, 101
- cultivation   95
- harvesting   95
melon   8, 84, 85, 100, 101
- cultivation   100
- fruit shapes   101
mixed crop   9, 23, 25, 29, 70
module   8, 12, 15, 17, 19, 21, 22, 24, 27, 34, 45,
46, 53, 64, 73, 75, 84, 89, 91, 91, 95, 122, 125
mulching   9, 46, 64, 84, 85, 89, 90, 92, 95, 99,
106
musk melons   101

New Zealand spinach   28, 29, 56, 57
- harvesting   57

oil marrow   94
okra   84, 96,
- cultivation   96
- harvesting   96
- uses   97
onions and related vegetables   116-126
- cultivation   116
- uses   117
orache   28, 56, 57
- cultivation   56
- harvesting   57
ornamental gourd   7, 94

Pak-choi   11, 26, 27
parsley   58, 62, 63, 66, 67, 116
- cultivation   63
- harvesting   63
- storing   63
parsnip   58, 66
- cultivation   66
- harvesting   66, 67
pearl onion   124, 125
peas   8, 108, 110
perforated plastic film   9, 10, 15, 24, 28, 30, 47,
59, 60, 69, 70, 71, 83, 102
Peruvian winter cherry   84, 106
- cultivation   106
- harvesting   107
- sowing   106
- uses   107
Plasmodiophora brassicae   11, 20

plastic film   9, 84, 87, 90, 100, 102, 106
plastic film mulch   102
plastic shelter   37
polytunnel   9, 18, 28, 30, 36, 59, 70, 92, 95, 99, 100, 106
potato   82
  - cultivation   83
  - harvesting   82, 83
  - sprouting tubers before planting   82
pregerminating   8
Psila rosae   60
pumpkin   94, 95
  - cultivation   95
purslane   40, 41
  - cultivation   41
  - harvesting   41

radish   23, 58, 59, 68, 69, 70
  - cultivation   68
  - forcing   69
  - harvesting   68
  - storing   68
rhubarb   28, 50, 51
  - cultivation   50
  - forcing   50
  - harvesting   50
root and tubers   7, 58-83
  - cultivation   58
  - forcing   59
  - harvesting   58
  - storing   59
root celery   64
root parsley   62, 63

salsify   58, 78, 79
  - harvesting   79
  - storing   79
Savoy cabbage   11, 14, 15
  - cultivation   15
  - forcing   14
scarlet runner beans   112
  - harvesting   113
scorsonera   58, 78, 79
  - cultivation   78
  - harvesting   78, 79
seed bed   8, 12, 17, 19, 21, 22, 30, 34, 124
shallots   116, 118, 119
  - harvesting   119
  - storing   119
shock of transplanting   46
small radish   8, 9, 19, 58, 59, 70, 71
  - cultivation   70
  - harvesting   70, 71

soil   6, 8
summer crisphead lettuce   30
sorts of peas   110
spaghetti marrow   94
spinach   28, 54, 55, 83
  - cultivation   55
  - forcing   55
  - harvesting   55
  - uses   55
sprouting broccoli   18, 19
storage pit   63, 66, 74, 78, 81
sugar beet   42
summer radish   68, 69
swede   58, 74, 75, 76
  - cultivation   75
  - harvesting   75
  - storing   74, 75
sweet corn   102, 103
  - cultivation   102
  - harvesting   102
sweet fennel   46
  - cultivation   46
  - harvesting   47
  - storing   47
sweet pepper   6, 8, 9, 84, 88, 89, 90, 97
  - cultivation   88, 89
  - harvesting   89
Swiss chard   28, 42, 43, 72
  - cultivation   42
  - harvesting   42
  - varieties   42
system of crop rotation   9

time of sowing   7, 8, 9
tomato   6, 8, 9, 84, 85, 86, 87, 97
  - cultivation   86
  - diversity of varieties   87
  - sowing   86
turnip   42, 58, 59, 75, 76
  - cultivation   76
  - harvesting   76
  - types   76, 77

watercress   28, 38, 39
  - cultivation   39
  - harvesting   39
watermelon   98, 100
  - cultivation   99
Welsh onion   120, 121
winter endive   35
winter radish   68, 69

zucchini   94